L.E.A.R.N.
EVANGELISM
HANDBOOK

L.E.A.R.N. Evangelism Handbook

Copyright © 2019 Dr. Marshall M. Windsor. All rights reserved.

Unless otherwise marked, all Scripture quotations are from the NIV, ESV and KJV of the Holy Bible. Public domain.

ISBN: 978-1-63308-489-6 (hardback)
978-1-63308-488-9 (paperback)
978-1-63308-490-2 (ebook)

Interior and Cover Design by R'tor John D. Maghuyop

CHALFANT ECKERT
PUBLISHING

1028 S Bishop Avenue, Dept. 178
Rolla, MO 65401

Printed in United States of America

L.E.A.R.N.
EVANGELISM
HANDBOOK

*Giving Away
The Greatest Gift*

Dr. Marshall M. Windsor

CHALFANT ECKERT

PUBLISHING

To Nancy

Truly, the love of my life

"You can laugh at Christianity, you can mock it and ridicule it. But it works. It changes lives, I should say Jesus Christ changes lives. Christianity is not religion; it's not a system; it's not an ethical idea; it's not a psychological phenomenon. It's a person. If you trust Christ, start watching your attitudes and actions because Jesus Christ is in the business of changing lives."

Josh McDowell
More Than A Carpenter
Living Books, 1986

TABLE OF CONTENTS

INTRODUCTION

One of the scariest words in the church today is the word *evangelism*. It seems to strike fear into so many hearts and keeps us from sharing "the hope that is within" each and every follower of Jesus Christ (1 Peter 3:15). Culture today has embraced tolerance to an unhealthy level; to the point of influencing Christians to abscond from the divine directives of our Lord and Savior, Jesus Christ—to "Go therefore and make disciples of all nations" (Matthew 28:19). The Scriptures give us some great insights into actively sharing our faith. The Apostle Paul shared one such Scripture:

> *Let your speech always be gracious,*
> *seasoned with salt, so that you may know*
> *how you ought to answer each person.*
> Colossians 4:6 (ESV)

Talking with people is obviously part of sharing our faith with others and doing so as the Bible advises is paramount to successfully presenting the truths of Scripture in ways that will be received.

Honestly, there are days when every Christian might struggle with his or her inadequacies in sharing the Gospel message. Social media has only heightened the human sensitivity to insecurities and fears of rejection; no one likes to be rejected or ridiculed. As a matter of fact, evangelism in any culture demands overcoming our fears by taking a step of faith to help someone escape the coming judgment of Christ (2 Timothy 4:1). We should all pray that the love of God would so fill our hearts that we could not help but share

God's wonderful news when opportunities to do so arise. As Greg Laurie shared in his book, *How to Share Your Faith,*

> "Any effective sharing of one's faith will always begin with a God-given burden! And if some of us today were brutally honest, we would have to say that we don't have that burden. If we did, quite frankly, I think many of us would do more than we do."[1]

May the Lord give us a sense of holy dissatisfaction when we cease sharing what God has done in our lives and the wonderful plan that God has for His creation.

I hope that this book will encourage you to get together with another believer or two and encourage yourselves in the Lord (1 Thessalonians 5:11) as you step out to scatter some Gospel seed. You can do it! As a matter of fact, the "Bible clearly teaches that personal witnessing is not restricted to a few who are especially gifted for evangelism."[2] In all honesty, personal evangelism is about starting conversations in hopes that you can share about the awesomeness of God and what He has done in your life, while sincerely listening to people who have genuine doubts and possible negative experiences. I am praying that *L.E.A.R.N. Evangelism* will help you get started towards initiating those spiritual conversations.

So, what is *L.E.A.R.N. Evangelism* anyway? *L.E.A.R.N. Evangelism* is merely a tool to encourage you to start conversations and share your faith. But remember, a conversation is a two-way street. We need to do as much—if not more—listening respectfully to others as we do in sharing what God has done in our lives. God

---

1   Greg Laurie, *How to Share Your Faith* (Carol Stream, IL: Tyndale House, 1999), 3.

2   Randy Hurst, *Response Evangelism* (Springfield, MO: Gospel Publishing House, 2005), 14.

longs to bring others into a right relationship with Him, and He may just want to use you to do that! There is no one way of sharing our faith that is fruitful in every situation; that is why the role of the Holy Spirit is so important. We all have a story about what God has done in our lives, and your story may just be *THE* story that helps change another person's life for eternity.

In this book, I hope that the Holy Spirit will also reveal the importance of building relationships with others. Sometimes, relationships are God's teaching tools in our own lives. Likewise, we need to be intentional in our personal relationships. The hope is to share Christ and reveal the difference He can make when a person invites Him into his or her life. So, take a deep breath, say fervent prayers for opportunities and the words to say, then step into a world waiting for you! Start building relationships and initiating discussions in hopes of sharing Christ with someone who does not know Him. Every Christian should pray for a special sensitivity to divine opportunities that the Lord may have orchestrated for just that moment. That said, we should all try to intentionally foster at least one new friend every year. Building relationships is a crucial key in discovering divine sharing opportunities.

In the following pages, I have incorporated the *L.E.A.R.N.* acronym into separate chapters, followed by deeper illustrations of outreach stories and opportunities that complement those key words. I've included some evangelism opportunities I encountered over the years that gave me the privilege of sharing a few Gospel seeds of encouragement. I pray that in the pages ahead, you too will find some encouragement concerning the privilege of sharing your faith journey with others. Seeing other people cross the line of faith in a sincere prayer of forgiveness and faith for salvation in Jesus Christ is an undeniable joy—I pray that you have opportunities to experience it often.

But first, we must all ask ourselves a very real—and revealing—question. Is sharing the Gospel message with others really worth the cost? Is it really so important that we should risk the rejection or affliction that may ensue? Are we willing to stand out—to be different? The next chapter tackles this legitimate question. It is adapted from an in-depth research paper on Jon Huss that I wrote a few years ago. That just means that there are a lot of references and details about Jon Huss that might go beyond the normal conversation. But as you read the following pages, I hope you'll gain an appreciation for all those Christians who have gone before us and suffered unimaginable consequences for their faith. Perhaps, it will help allay your personal fears about faith conversations and reveal opportunities that you had overlooked.

CHAPTER 1

IS IT REALLY WORTH IT?

There are some days when I wonder if I'm doing any good at all with my faith—or my Christianity. When I see the blatant rejection and persecution of Christians today it causes me to ask myself, "Are we really making any difference at all?" But it stands to reason, the mere fact that persecution still occurs seems to only validate the need to sow additional Gospel seed. You never know the life that Jesus is getting ready to change by your obedience. But sadly, I also realize that the thought of potential rejection and persecution gives rise to anxiety in many of us.

> "As the flames leap higher, one can see a man tied to a stake in the midst of this fiery ordeal…"

That's why faith is so important. I recently read that "faith thrives in holy discomfort,"[3] which seems to have a ring of truth about it. We have to take a step of faith whenever we share words of hope with someone we may or may not know well, because that causes a bit of holy discomfort in most of us. Paul encourages us in Romans 10:17 with this promise, "So faith comes from hearing,

---

3   Louie Giglio, *Goliath Must Fall: Winning the Battle Against Your Giants* (Nashville, TN: W. Publishing, 2017), 115.

and hearing through the word of God." That's why reading the Scripture and spending time with God are so important—it helps us become people of faith who can overcome our fears in order to follow Christ's commands.

But is overcoming your fears about possible rejection and ridicule really worth it when it comes to talking about your faith journey? Can one person really make a difference for the Kingdom of God? I submit to you that we will all face our fears and be confronted with challenges if we endeavor to be true disciples of Jesus Christ. When we seek to follow Christ with all of our hearts, souls, and minds, we'll find ourselves slowly changed into His likeness—even though in part on this side of heaven. As the Apostle Paul stated in 2 Corinthians 3:18 (KJV),

But we all, with open face beholding as in a glass the glory of the Lord, are changed into the same image from glory to glory, even as by the Spirit of the Lord.

As we submit to the commands of Scripture and strive to follow the leading of the Holy Spirit, there is no telling the impact that we can have on our friends, family, peers, communities, and even generations to come. In the pages that follow, I want to share a story about a man whose legacy still effects generations today through his unwavering faith to God and willingness to stand in the face of adversity for the sake of the Gospel. Our story begins in the fourteenth century, through a son of peasants, who would help change the world.

A Man Called John Huss

As the flames leap higher one can see a man tied to a stake in the midst of this fiery ordeal. A paper crown has been placed upon his head with images of demons, labeling him the heretic of all heretics by the inscription "The Archheretic."[4] But one must remember this is the fifteenth century and heretics were frequently burned at the stake for blasphemy of any kind towards the Catholic Church. And not the Catholic Church as one would think of it today—a Church accomplishing so much good and introducing untold masses to Jesus Christ. This was a politically powerful church with authority to depose emperors. To see one burned at the stake was not an uncommon sight, but to see the innocent killed was an altogether different story.

The occasion seems to be indeed different, and undoubtedly a different kind of man, as singing comes from the midst of the flames. This man, John Huss, continues to sing as the flames of death leap higher, consuming clothes and flesh in its path. Huss sings a familiar hymn, "Christ, Thou Son of the Living God, have mercy upon me."[5] His apparent victory in death seems to be cut short when starting the third verse, as a gust of wind blows the flames up into his face, ending even the most determined attempt at life. And so, the beginning of the end has once again come to pass. Was this just another heretic burned at the stake, or a martyr of the true faith, who stood for the truth of God's Holy Word?

The date is July 6, 1415 in the beautiful city of Constance, Switzerland. King Sigismund of Germany had called a council to end the divisions that were currently in the Catholic Church, namely, that there were three Popes. Each one fighting for control and using whatever means available to do so. The Council lasted over three years, with the martyrdom of Huss as one of its answers to the problem of heretical teaching, or so they thought. Out of his martyrdom grew the Church of the Bohemian Brethren, which was a catalyst for the Reformation. Even John Wesley, was influenced

---

4   J. P. Bartak, *John Hus at Constance* (Nashville: Cokesbury Press, 1979), 52.

5   Ibid., 55.

by this man from Bohemia three centuries later in his Methodist movement. Wesley's movement became seed for the Pentecostal movement, which Pentecostals saw as the complete restoration of the New Testament Church, at the turn of the twentieth century.

The life and martyrdom of John Huss had a dramatic impact upon the Church of the fifteenth century. So much so, that John Huss continued to have an influence after his death upon Martin Luther's beliefs in the Protestant Reformation of the sixteenth century, and Pentecostal organizations today. Let us begin by taking a look at Huss' journey from Husinec to the Council of Constance. We'll also exam some of Huss' influences, those he influenced, and major issues that have been passed down through the centuries.

The Forming of a Martyr

The actual date of birth for John Huss is unknown, but the best guess is 1373. Some have speculated it to be 1369, but this would mean that Huss received his ordination at the age of thirty-two, instead of the more normative age of twenty-five. John Huss was born in the small village of Husinec, which was located in the southern part of Bohemia (a small country that is now a part of the Czech Republic), and had a population of approximately 1,800 people. Even the actual day of his birth is a mystery, and the tradition of July 6 being celebrated as his birthday may really be just the remembrance of the day he was burned at the stake. The term "birthday" for the Hussites actually meant the day someone died, "since death for them was the birth to the life of the spirit."[6]

---

6   Paul Roubiczek and Joseph Kalmer, *Warrior of God: The Life and Death of John Hus* (London: Nicholson and Watson, 1947), 22.

The name John Huss, also spelled Jan Hus, is a little misleading because Huss was not really his last name, nor do we know his real last name. It was not uncommon to associate one's name to the village or town where they lived or were born. John Huss often signed his name "John Hus" and some official documents were signed "as Magister or even Doctor Johannes of Husinecz."[7] The Czech word "hus" actually meant goose, which made John Huss the brunt of many a joke, mainly by his own doing. On one occasion when a friend wrote about his last name, Huss replied, "If you love your poor Goose, see to it that the king sends him guards."[8]

Little is also known of Huss' early life as a boy growing up in Husinec. His parents were apparently peasants, with his father dying at an early age. John seemed to be his mother's favorite and she was adamant about getting him an education and becoming a priest. So much so that she would accompany him to school at times. His mother's apparent standard of a godly home seemed to be reflected in Huss' character, which was never brought into question during any period of his life. Huss also thought highly of his mother and credits her with teaching him to say, "Amen, may God grant it."[9] John did have other siblings but nothing significant is really known about any of them.

John Huss had the best education of his times, but it was definitely not handed to him on a silver platter. Huss initially attended the local monastery school in Husinec, and when they saw his potential the monks sent him to the school in nearby Prachatice. He did very well there and upon completion decided that he was

---

7   David S. Schaff, *John Huss: His Life, Teachings, and Death* (New York, Charles Scribner's Sons, 1915), 19.

8   Ibid., 20.

9   Matthew Spinka, *John Hus: A Biography* (New Jersey: Princeton University Press, 1968), 22.

going to the University of Prague. Surely his arrival in the large city of Prague was a shock to Huss, coming from such a small country town. Prague's population was approximately eighty thousand people in 1389, with approximately seven thousand belonging to the University of Prague "according to very cautious estimates."[10]

Coming from a somewhat poor background, Huss had to work his way through college. He tells of a time in which he had "to add to his limited means by acting as singing boy at religious services."[11] The scarcity of money is evident as Huss tells of a time while in school that he made a spoon out of bread, and after he had eaten his peas, "he ate the spoon also."[12] There were times when the ground was his only bed as he quickly came to the realization that since he was from a peasant background he would have to start at the very bottom of the social and academic ladder. He was eventually allowed to get room and board in one of his professor's homes, in exchange for services rendered. The farther up the scholastic ladder one was, the better accommodations could be gained in exchange for keeping the professor's rooms in order.

John Huss was influenced by several people, two of which were even from his own school in Prachatice, while studying at the University of Prague. These two men were Christian and Nicholas of Prachatice, who had preceded Huss by approximately five years. Christian must have truly taken John Huss under his wing as Huss continually referred to him as his "benefactor" throughout his ministry. John Huss' teachers were also influential in forming his thinking along the lines of John Wyclif, since they were predominately followers of Wyclif's realism philosophy. And

---

10 Roubiczek and Kalmer, 21.

11 W. N. Schwarze, *John Hus, The Martyr of Bohemia* (New York: Fleming H. Revell Co, 1915), 29.

12 Schaff, 21.

the writings of John Wyclif themselves were probably the strongest influences in John Huss' thinking. However, Huss did not agree with everything Wyclif said, "but always tested critically how far they affected essential orthodoxy."[13]

John Huss received his Bachelor of Arts degree in 1393, his Bachelor of Divinity in 1394, and his Master of Arts in 1396. Following these achievements, Huss began teaching in the area of the Arts in 1396. On March 14, 1402, John Huss was appointed as "rector and preacher of the Bethlehem Chapel,"[14] also known as the Holy Innocents at Bethlehem. It was not until this appointment that Huss actually received an "adequate income" for his work. Huss himself was initially overjoyed at the monetary benefits of priesthood, but later confessed that his initial reason for pursuit of the priesthood was to have the best clothes, food, and condiments that society could provide.

It was here at Bethlehem Chapel, that John Huss began to preach what others in the Catholic Church would call heresy. The Bethlehem Chapel was built and devoted to the preaching of the Gospel in the people's language, which was contrary to the standard of the Catholic Church at the time. The Catholic Church conducted all services in Latin, and considered all laity as being too ignorant to understand the Scriptures anyway. The strategic location of the Chapel within the great metropolitan city of Prague made it a tremendous epicenter for dispersing the true Gospel as Huss saw it.

Huss was a man without fear as he chastised clergy and others who showed "indifference to the spiritual needs of the people,"[15] as well as those in blatant sin. Huss had scathing words for those who dared to be called clergy yet stain their position by immorality,

---

13 Spinka, 37.

14 Ibid., 39.

15 Schaff, 36.

including the Pope. A typical theme of John Huss, and among later reformers, was that of "Christ riding on a donkey and the pope on a stallion with the people crowding to kiss his feet."[16] This was all because John Huss had a heart for the people and their spiritual needs. From the poor to the rich, he could relate and sympathize with them all.

Initially, Huss preached the standard "orthodox" Catholic sermons in the people's language, even though he wrote them in Latin. But as the years passed by, he began to lean more to the teachings of John Wyclif. The primary arguments Huss had against the Catholic Church were the abuses of authority, the "substitution of rites and ceremonies for heart-religion,"[17] as well as the selling of spiritual favors or benefits for financial gain, otherwise known as indulgences. Pope John XXIII demonstrated this when he told the people that he "gave full remission of sins to all those who would war on his side to defend the Church."[18]

The three main institutions or areas of medieval thought that Huss attacked were the absolute authority of the papacy, the sacramental Church, and the inquisition,[19] which stated that a heretic did not even have the right to live. Huss did not believe that the papacy had supreme authority above the Scriptures, or over persons, to include the authority to depose emperors, and dispense life or death. He also did not believe that clergy living in sin should be allowed to serve the sacraments, even though he believed transubstantiation (the belief that the bread and wine served at communion literally became the body and blood of Christ upon consecration—only

---

16   Roland H. Bainton, *Christianity* (New York: Houghton Mifflin Co., 1987), 217.

17   Levi Oscar Kuhns, *John Huss: The Witness* (Cincinnati: Jennings and Graham, 1907), 11.

18   W. Grinton Berry, *Foxe's Book of Martyrs* (Grand Rapids: Baker Books, 1994), 93.

19   Schaff, 4.

the appearance of bread and wine remained) still took place. The sacramental Church position of the Catholic Church believed that "no matter how immoral the priest may be, his words accomplish the transubstantiation of the bread and wine."[20] And Huss believed the inquisition itself was just a means for removing those who disagreed with the Catholic Church. He preached his opposition to all three of these "institutions" in some form or another.

Upon Huss' continued preaching of this so-called "heresy," the Pope issued an order that he should be excommunicated and that all preaching by him be stopped immediately. Huss continued to preach and the order to pull down Bethlehem Chapel was given. This created quite the uproar and John Huss, after much prayer, decided to go into exile. King Wenceslaus had asked him to leave and some nobles in southern Bohemia offered to provide protection for him. Huss visited his Church in Prague intermittently, but whenever he tried to preach the officials would stop the services because, "it was hard for them to hear the Word of God,"[21] Huss said.

The Council of Constance

The Council of Constance had been needed for several years before it actually materialized. The incident with John Huss was not the driving reason for the Council and happened to be more incidental than anything else. The issues of heresy were always of concern within the Catholic Church, and the Church had already tried to end the believed heretical teachings of John Huss to no avail. Predominate reasons for the Council of Constance included

---

20   Schaff, 8.

21   Spinka, 164.

addressing the embarrassing situation of immorality within the clergy, as well as repairing the schism that was currently within the Catholic Church involving three Popes.

The Council of Constance finally deposed all three existing Popes and appointed Martin V, under the name of Pope John XXIII, as the single Pope in order to reunite the Church. The additional task before the Council was "the extermination of heresy and a reformation of the Church in head and members."[22] John Huss was one of three cases heard and his trial revolved around "39 Articles," the majority of them being from his book, *De Ecclesia* (The Church).

By the time Huss arrived in Constance, Michael de Causis and Stephen Palecz had already posted many ludicrous lies about him in order to stir up the people. Many were merely products of their own imaginations, one of which was that Huss claimed to be "the fourth person added to the Trinity."[23] Stephen Palecz, who at one time was one of Huss' closest friends, was now one of his greatest enemies. Even Martin Luther, a century later, described the Council as a bunch of "wild boars," when referring to their dealings with John Huss.

One problem John Huss had was that the Council already viewed him as being condemned, so in the eyes of the Council he had no rights at all. To the Council, Huss was "assumed to be a liar and treated as one."[24] John Huss neither realized this perspective of the Council, nor did he realize that he stood "before a tribunal that had already reached its verdict."[25] And although King Sigismund,

---

22 Matthew Spinka, *John Hus: at the Council of Constance* (New York: Columbia University Press, 1965), 65.

23 Bartak, 40.

24 Spinka, *John Hus: at the Council of Constance*, 74.

25 P. De Vooght, "Hus, John," vol. 7 of *New Catholic Encyclopedia* (New York: McGraw-Hill, 1967), 272.

King Wenceslaus' brother, promised John Huss safe travels, it was a promise he could not keep. It took almost a year to convict Huss, with the results seeing him burned at the stake. His time spent over that period of his life in Constance was one of sickness, pain, and loneliness. But John Huss was ever thinking about his church, not himself, and wrote many letters during his imprisonment at Constance before he died.

A Seed of The Reformation

One cannot talk of John Huss without mentioning the Hussites and the Hussite wars, which unified a country but ended in the death of thousands. The flames in Constance were intended to extinguish the teachings of John Huss, but they only served to ignite the hearts of a people ready for reform. The Hussites were comprised of two main groups: The "Calixtines (sometimes called the Utraquists)"[26] which were the conservative party comprised of the nobility, and the Taborites which were the radicals mainly comprised of peasants. The Taborite army was extremely fierce and enemies would run in fear at their approach. Another Bohemian group also arose that did not take up arms to fight but resolved to follow more closely the example of John Huss. They gathered together in 1457 from every class of people and eventually called themselves "the Unity of the Brethren (*Unitas Fratrum*)."[27]

After Huss' death, the Hussites created the Four Articles of Prague in 1419. These were their doctrinal beliefs, largely from the teachings of John Huss. These were:

---

26 Kuhns, 146.

27 Schwarze, 147.

1) The Word of God is to be preached freely; 2) The sacrament of the body and blood of Christ is to be served in the form of both bread and wine to all faithful Christians; 3) Priests are to relinquish earthly position and possessions, and all are to begin an obedient life based on the apostolic model; and 4) All public sins are to be punished and public sinners in all positions are to be restrained.[28]

Regaining "the cup" of the sacrament, which the Church had taken away, was a major goal of the Hussites. The Church had limited the cup to the clergy alone, "lest the clumsy laity should spill any of the 'blood of God'."[29] These Articles were the words that the Hussites lived and died by, and which they took with them to the Council of Basel in 1432, when asked to attend as partners of the Council, in order to defend their position. It was then that they were officially recognized as an independent institution, although more in lip service than anything else.

The Catholic Church organized more than one attempt to staunch the rebellious Czechs, with nothing to show for their efforts except the death of thousands of their own men. Greed eventually won the day when the Utraquists accepted payment to wipe out the Taborites from John Palomar, a member of the Council that had convened at Prague. A decisive battle was fought at the town of Lipany, and the Taborites "were decimated in ferocious carnage."[30] What others could not do the Czechs did to themselves, with some thirteen thousand killed.

---

28 Jan Milic Lochman, *Living Roots of Reformation* (Minneapolis: Augsburg, 1979), 79-84.

29 Bainton, 217.

30 Spinka, *John Hus: A Biography*, 317.

Scarcely one hundred years and many martyrs later, a man named Martin Luther (1483-1546) arose to the challenge of reformation. The thinking of John Huss is clearly seen in the actions of Luther during this reformation period of the Church. It was Martin Luther who took a stand against Rome in 1517 and nailed his ninety-five theses "against indulgences to the door of the Castle Church,"[31] located in the Saxony town of Wittenburg. In 1516, Pope Leo X had offered more indulgences to pay for his supposed imminent war with the Turks. He said that for anyone who would give at least ten shillings, he would, "at his pleasure deliver one soul from the pains of purgatory."[32] Like Huss, Luther saw the selling of indulgences by the Catholic Church to raise money for individual agendas as unscriptural, and that the Pope was not above Scripture.

Martin Luther was a German Catholic monk in the Augustine order, who slowly began to see the truth of Huss' teachings while studying the Bible. While a student, Luther had many of Huss' sermons and out of curiosity began reading the teachings of the supposed heretic. Luther was "moved with admiration" and also surprised that someone "so apt and so serious in expounding the Scriptures should have been burned as a heretic."[33] In 1520, Luther asked the Roman Church to confess its error in burning Huss, to no avail. One year later Luther recanted his earlier statement that only some of Huss' articles were true at Constance. He now insisted they were indeed "all true," and that the pope and papists had now replaced the Gospel with "the doctrines of the dragon of hell."[34]

---

31 Edward Langton, *History of the Moravian Church* (London: George Allen and Unwin Ltd., 1956), 41.

32 Berry, 156.

33 Schaff, 292.

34 Ibid., 294.

Martin Luther had obviously drawn the line after this blatant denunciation of the Catholic Church, and especially her leaders.

By the time Martin Luther appeared, "the *Unitas Fratrum* embraced about four hundred parishes and two hundred thousand members."[35] The primary excellence of this Church was in the area of evangelism and strict discipline. Bible-based schools and seminaries arose as the need for education was exposed, in order to eradicate any ignorance that might lead one back to sin or errors in doctrine. The United Brethren Church was the first Church to put hymnbooks into the hands of the people, in their own language, with the first printing dated 1501.

Martin Luther became more involved with the United Brethren as he was forced to defend his writings at the Leipzig disputation in 1519. After his defense, many letters of support and encouragement arrived from these brothers in the faith whom he had not even met. The United Brethren even sent representatives to talk with Luther in 1522, encouraging him and sharing with him their own beliefs. When the United Brethren Church sent Luther a copy of their constitution and doctrines in 1523, it was noted that "he was well pleased,"[36] even though he initially did not care for these people. There were several occasions when the United Brethren sent representatives to meet with Luther, and on every occasion admonished him to implement a system of strict discipline. It was in 1536 that Luther felt he could no longer continue with the United Brethren due to their persistence in the area of Church discipline.

The United Brethren sincerely embraced Martin Luther throughout his lifetime, even with their different views of discipline, as well as Calvin and others. The continued close

---

35   Schwarze, 149.

36   Kuhns, 167.

relationship between Luther's movement and the United Brethren was evidenced in 1570, when the United Brethren "formed with the Lutherans and Reformed of Poland"[37] for an evangelical alliance that was unprecedented for its time. And even today the United Brethren continue to live on, in what is known as the Moravian Church.

Martin Luther often, and repeatedly, gave John Huss credit for being a great witness and influence in his life. Martin Luther shared his own insight of Huss in a letter written to his friend George Spalatin in Altenberg on June 23, 1520: "I have hitherto taught and held all the opinions of John Hus unawares; so did John Staupitz: in short, we all are Hussites to a word."[38] Luther talks of Huss as a man somewhat before his time and that Luther, himself, was as well. Martin Luther reflected upon the supreme influence of Huss by stating his opinion that, "John Huss bought with his own blood the Gospel which we now possess."[39]

There is no question that John Huss made a lasting impression on Martin Luther and the Reformation of the sixteenth century. The seemingly prophetic words of John Huss seem to ring true when he said, "A hundred years hence you shall answer for this before God and me,"[40] as he had boldly told his accusers at the Council of Constance. A 1572 Hussite hymnal also reveals to us the influence of Wyclif upon Huss and Huss upon Luther. A picture inside the hymnal reveals Wyclif striking flints to start a fire, while Huss appears to be actually starting the fire and Martin Luther is holding up a "burning torch."

---

37 Schwarze, 150.

38 J. P. Bartak, 52.

39 Kuhns, 171.

40 Langton, 41.

Threads of Huss Today

Even through the thirty years war, which almost wiped out the United Brethren Church in 1618-1648, a "Hidden Seed"[41] remained. It was this "hidden seed" that found its way to Herrnhut in Saxony to begin the building process of the "brethren" once again. Since many of these people came from Moravia, the name given to this reformation of the United Brethren, was that of the Moravian Church. The Moravian Church was dedicated to aggressive missionary works and extensive travel, as seen by John Wesley's meetings with them on several occasions.

Wesley was greatly influenced by these German Moravian missionaries while aboard a ship bound for America, and later by another missionary named Peter Bohler. Bohler taught Wesley that "saving faith brought with it both dominion over sin and true peace of mind."[42] And who can forget the "heartwarming" experience that John Wesley felt as he learned from these Moravians. The very people that influenced his beliefs of Holiness, tradition, and experience coupled with the love and grace of God that allows us to come to him with simple child-like faith. Over three hundred years after his death, these Moravians were still carrying the lamp that John Huss lit. And it was the Moravians that had such a profound impact upon Wesley's beliefs regarding holiness and the second blessing, now regarded as the Baptism in the Holy Spirit.

It was largely John Wesley's beliefs that played a major part in the history of the Assemblies of God fellowship; and his Methodist movement became a major contributor to Pentecostal beliefs in the nineteenth and twentieth centuries. John Wesley had learned

---

41 Schwarze, 150.

42 Vinson Synan, *The Holiness Pentecostal Tradition: Charismatic Movements in the Twentieth Century* (Grand Rapids: Eerdmans, 1971), 4.

about justification by faith alone from Peter Bohler, as well as the awareness of safety and assurance that accompanied this faith. Bohler told Wesley that, "if you have not the assurance, you have not the faith."[43] Wesley was also highly impressed by their piety and walk of holiness. It was John Wesley who helped regain the "heart religion" that was so desperately needed.

We cannot say that everything we believe, or practice was a direct result of John Huss' thinking, but he has no doubt indirectly influenced many of our practices today. Evangelical churches believe, like John Huss, that the Scriptures are inspired by God and that they alone should be used to interpret other Scriptures, as well as be the supreme guide for us in matters of faith and doctrine. John Huss repeatedly told the Council at Constance that if they could show him where he erred in the Scriptures, he would gladly recant any of his teachings. John Huss was a man who did not hold himself above correction—a position that should be embraced by every person of faith today.

So, we see that the thread of John Huss is rather long as we look back through history. Many characteristics of his thinking have been passed down through the centuries, with some historians noting that most reformers, "accepted the doctrine of inspiration and, by implication, the doctrine of inerrancy"[44] espoused by Huss. This aspect of Huss' teaching can be seen today in the Church's stand for the authority of Scripture, its inspiration, and infallibility. All because of one man's unwavering faith and willingness to confront his fears and share the truth.

---

43   C. T. Winchester, *The Life of John Wesley* (New York: Macmillan, 1906), 55.

44   The Assemblies of God, *Where We Stand* (Springfield: Gospel Publishing House, 1989), 9.

So, What Do You Think?

As we have looked back across the life of John Huss, we see a man of extraordinary strength. Strength to stand for what he believed was right, moral, and everlasting. A strength that could not have been completely his own, but divinely apportioned unto him. A strength that grew out of his love for the people and for the truth of Scripture coupled with an unrelenting relationship with his savior, Jesus Christ. A strength that spread out of one of the smallest countries in the world but touched the lives of millions. In John Huss we see once again that God does not always call those equipped for the task, but He equips those who answer his call.

So, what do you think? Was it worth someone giving the small pamphlet to John Huss's father? An item that seemed meaningless to many became a vital link to restoring a young boy's relationship with God; and charted a course that continues to impact generations. John Huss' greatest contribution to the reformation of the Church was his thinking. His way of thinking and interpretation of Scripture changed the thinking of all that heard him preach. And as an artery pumps blood to every part of the body, all the people represented in Prague began to take the thinking of John Huss back to their respective countries, planting more seeds of reformation. Seeds that would fall to the ground and die, in order to bring about reformation.

Was it worth it for John Huss? Overcoming his own fears and eventually being martyred for his faith? A faith that stood for the truth in the face of extreme adversity. There is no question that John Huss inspired the people of his homeland and beyond by his willingness to suffer death for the Gospel. Even the early third century theologian, Tertullian, knew that the blood of all the Christians through the ages was really the harvest seed of the Church, and when one seed is planted, the harvest of that seed multiplies. And as one martyr dies and inspires many others, so we are inspired today by the persecution of those who have gone before us spreading the truth of the Gospel of our Lord Jesus Christ.

John Huss was a man who lived and died by the sword of God's Word. A sword so sharp that it divides the soul from the spirit, and the wheat from the tares (Matthew 13:30). As John Huss was led to martyrdom, you cannot help but remember that Jesus himself was led like a lamb to slaughter (Isaiah 53:5-7). Enduring the cross but despising its shame, for you and for me. The price for our spiritual liberty has come with a dear price. It's also a price for whom many are unaware today unless we share with them this wonderful news. May we ever remember the last words John Huss sang, as the hungry flames slowly ended his life: "Christ, Thou Son of the living God, have mercy upon me."[45]

So, is it really worth it? I think so and I pray the chapters ahead will embolden you in some small way to take a step of faith in starting faith conversations that will start changing your world. I want to encourage you and let you know that God has been wanting to use you more than you can imagine. When you have a right relationship with God, you have all the resources you need to step out and make a positive difference in someone else's life. You can do this. You're a child of the King! So, let the Holy Spirit of God light your candle of faith so that you, in turn, can go and help change the world—one soul at a time.

---

45 Bartak, 55.

Go Light Your World[46]

There is a candle in every soul
Some brightly burning, some dark and cold
There is a Spirit who brings a fire
Ignites a candle and makes His home

So, carry your candle, run to the darkness
Seek out the hopeless, confused and torn
Hold out your candle for all to see it
Take your candle, and go light your world
Take your candle, and go light your world

---

46   *Go Light Your World* was written by Kathy Troccoli in 1995. There are three additional
verses.

CHAPTER 2

LISTEN

L.E.A.R.N. Evangelism means to:

LISTEN – Listen to the whisper of the Holy Spirit.

It is crucial that you try your very best to sense God's gentle nudges through the leading of the Holy Spirit and reading of God's Word. This may seem like trying to hear someone whisper in the midst of a storm because life can get so busy! But it is worth seeking the heart of our heavenly Father. The wonderful man of prayer George Mueller once said:

> I never remember, in all my Christian course, a period now (in March, 1895) of sixty-nine years and four months, that I ever sincerely and patiently sought to know the will of God by the teaching of the Holy Spirit, through the instrumentality of the Word of God, but I have been always directed rightly. But if honesty of heart and uprightness before God were lacking, or if I did not patiently wait upon God for instruction, or if I preferred the counsel of my

fellow men to the declarations of the Word of the living God, I made great mistakes.[47]

So, find a place and time to read the Scripture, seek the Lord in prayer, and ask Him to provide opportunities wherein you can share what God has done in your life.

As you listen in your times of prayer or even throughout the day, you may sense the Holy Spirit nudging you to share a particular thought with a person you are with or to talk with a specific person. There are people waiting and hoping that someone has answers to issues in their lives. Thankfully, God continues to use divine encounters if we will just listen to, and obey, the Holy Spirit's leading (John 16:13). When visiting with a person, remember to make sure you are attentive and listening to them. This says, "I care about how you feel and what you are saying is important." David Augsburger shared a great truth about this in Peter Scazzero's book, *The Emotionally Healthy Church*: "Being heard is so close to being loved that for the average person, they are almost indistinguishable."[48] That is why listening—to the Holy Spirit and the person you are talking to—is so important. The fact that the letters in "listen" can also be used to spell the word "silent" seems fitting. I admit though, that trying to do all of that listening and maintaining sensitivity to the Holy Spirit can be a real challenge! But that's exactly what I experienced on a flight that demanded a listening ear and the Holy Spirit's guiding hand.

On my flight from Providence to Chicago, I sat next to a lady named Sheila. She was a counselor from the Chicago area who

---

47   George Mueller, *Answers to Prayer*, compiled by A.E.C. Brooks, (Chicago, IL: Moody Press, 1984), 2.

48   Peter Scazzero with Warren Bird, *The Emotionally Healthy Church: A Strategy for Discipleship that Actually Changes Lives* (Grand Rapids: Zondervan, 2003), 181.

had become a Buddhist and had just been at a retreat for those who taught meditation techniques. I knew right then that it would be an interesting conversation and that I probably would not be celebrating any conversion victory stories like we often read about in all those evangelism books! But Sheila loved to talk, so I listened and inserted a few things about God and how God had really helped turn me around—how I enjoyed meditating on the Scriptures— just little things that I felt the Holy Spirit prompt me to share. I do remember mentioning at one point how I was amazed that God really did want to have a relationship with us and be involved in our lives.

Actually, I didn't really have a clue as to what I should say and was praying rather fervently along the lines of "God, if you want me to share something here I really wish you would start helping me, because I don't have a clue where to start with someone who is adamantly Buddhist!" As Sheila and I visited, I felt like the Holy Spirit shared with me that I just might be the person God wanted to use to help show Sheila that not every Christian was the way she had perceived them. Perhaps the Lord would use our conversation to help Sheila be a little more open whenever God really began to deal with her about her relationship with Him. Maybe I was link number one or two or three in her spiritual chain of who-knows-how-many. Thinking like that about our conversation really took a lot of pressure off of me, and I could just be myself without worrying about the outcome—that was God's responsibility.

But I was concerned that I was not able to share the Gospel with her per se and felt the Holy Spirit prompt me to ask her a question towards the end of our flight (I was looking for an opportunity but felt kind of nervous if the truth be known). So, I asked Sheila if she had any spiritual background prior to becoming a Buddhist (She had been talking about how her sect of Buddhism was very open to other faiths, etc.). She said that she grew up Catholic and attended a Catholic high school. We kidded each other about how strict that must have been, and we both admitted that we were not the tamest kids in school growing up. I felt relieved that she at least KNEW about Jesus if she had been in a Catholic school, but I told her that it was a pretty far stretch to go from being a Catholic to a Buddhist. We ended our conversation on a great note and went on our ways when the plane landed.

I needed the Holy Spirit to guide me, because I did not know Sheila or her faith path, but I knew that God wanted me to let Him use me however He thought best. You don't have to know all the right answers, you just have to be a willing vessel for the Lord's use. That's why faith is so important—we must believe that God can use anything we might know to help someone come to know Him more. An old saying in the church that I hope you take to heart goes like this, "God doesn't call the equipped, He equips those He calls."

In my situation with Sheila, I knew that I needed to exercise my faith and rely on the Holy Spirit to bring Scriptures to remembrance and questions that might help our discussion. I realized that whenever we find ourselves talking with others about the Gospel, man-made sales pitches and manipulative tactics scream ineffectiveness. As Rebecca Pippert shared:

I believe that much of our evangelism is ineffective because we depend too much upon technique and strategy. Evangelism has slipped into the sales department. I am convinced that we must look at Jesus, and the quality of life he calls us to, as a model for what to believe and how to reach out to others.[49]

---

49   Rebecca Manley Pippert, *Out of the Salt-Shaker & Into The World: evangelism as a way of life* (Downers Grove: InterVarsity, 1979), 13.

In order to do that I needed to believe that God would help me in my divine encounter with Sheila—and that's called faith. Being a bearer of good news, which is what Jesus Christ gives, demands divine guidance, faith, and intervention. God alone transforms lives and we need Him to lead and guide our faith conversations. Our prayer should be that God would use us to help others become thirsty for more of what we have within these earthen vessels—the Holy Spirit. Let me share with you about a man who knew how to walk in faith—even through the most difficult circumstances—in order to follow the Lord's command to share the Gospel.

A Man Who Knew How to Exercise Faith

Hudson Taylor started his life in 1832, at Barnsley, England. He found the Lord as a young boy one Saturday afternoon while reading one of his father's books. Miles away his mother was burdened to pray for him, and she did so until peace finally came. Upon her arrival home, she found her son unable to contain his excitement about his new-found Savior. Unknown to Hudson, his sister had been praying too. When he found out, Hudson and his sister joined together to zealously begin winning others to Christ. Hudson was only seventeen at the time.

As Hudson continued to grow in the Lord and spend hours before Him, he gained a sense that there was indeed a calling on his life. He said at one point, "For what service I was accepted I knew not; but a deep consciousness that I was no longer my own took possession of me, which has never since been effaced."[50] It was at one such time as he sought God, that the presence of God

---

50   J. Hudson Taylor, *A Retrospect*, 3rd ed. (Toronto, CA: China Inland Mission, 1902), 8.

overcame him and seemed to say to him that his petition had been answered. He said, "the impression was wrought into my soul that it was in China the Lord wanted me."[51] Hudson immediately began to prepare himself by exercising, ridding himself of every nicety he had, and studying Chinese. This last endeavor he accomplished with only a copy of the Gospel of Luke in Chinese. Hudson would compare short portions of Scripture to their counterpart in English to learn the challenging language of the Chinese.

Hudson would also come to the conclusion that prayer would be paramount in his success. "I thought to myself, 'When I get out to China, I shall have no claim on any one for anything; my only claim will be on God. How important, therefore, to learn before leaving England to move man, through God, by prayer alone.'"[52] What a great lesson for us all as we step out to share the wonderful message of hope with others.

As Hudson continued his preparations, he pursued an opportunity to become a physician's assistant that had presented itself in the town of Hull. But he was surrounded by luxuries in his new position, so he moved into a one-room cottage in the poor section of town known as "Drainside." It was in this place that Hudson faced lonely days of solitude and a broken heart, as he found that his love in life could not accompany him in his ventures to China, nor would her father hear of it. And though the tempter tried his best, Hudson found that the Lord indeed was a very present help in time of need as he drew ever closer to his Lord.

Hudson then moved to London and was accepted to medical school, and while there, God opened the door unexpectedly to China. When Hudson was twenty-one, the Chinese Evangelization Society asked him to go to Shanghai as soon as possible. The Taiping

---

51   J. Hudson Taylor, *A Retrospect*, 8.

52   Ibid., 14.

Rebellion had reached its climax, and their Christian leader wrote to a trusted American missionary saying, "bring with you many teachers to help in making known the truth."[53]

In 1854, Hudson arrived in China after a perilous five-month-long journey. The conditions that met him there were far from encouraging, as well as the bitter cold and lack of money to buy the expensive coal available. Hudson found himself struggling just to gain a foothold in Shanghai, much less anywhere inland. But in the first two years, Hudson Taylor was still able to make at least ten evangelistic journeys to the interior. He would travel by boat during the day, preaching wherever he could, and then return to the boat to study, pray, and sleep for the night. Hudson even adopted the Chinese dress in order to aid him in access to the people. It was here in China that Hudson met his first wife, Miss Dyer.

By 1860, Hudson Taylor had to return home due to illness. He went to Brighton for a break and to aid in recovery, when the Lord began beckoning him again. God wanted him to call for others to enlist with him that they might go to China for him. He started a bank account for the China Inland Mission with fifty dollars and began writing its publication, *China's Spiritual Need and Claims*. The China Inland Mission would send out missionaries believing the Lord would help them in their support.

Their first voyage with sixteen people and four children almost found them at the bottom of the China Sea as typhoon after typhoon swept over them for fifteen days. But their testimony to the crew during this period won the conversion of a large majority. They were initially able to reside in the town of Hangchow before branching out into other towns further inland. After sixteen months in Hangchow, Hudson and his family lived on boats for

---

53 Howard Taylor, *Hudson Taylor in Early Years: The Growth of A Soul* (New York: Hodder & Stoughton, 1912), 173.

two months as they headed toward Nanking but stopped in the city of Yangchow. Anonymous handbills accused foreigners of many things, including the stealing of children. Fire was set to their home and the missionaries were forced to leave; only the hand of God saved them from death. But God gained the final victory as doors where actually opened wider when they were finally allowed to return to Yangchow.

In the summer of 1870, the time had come to part with their children. There were no nearby schools to further their education and the climate and hardships of this life had already taken its toll. One of their little ones was already in the grave. Their secretary and friend Miss Emily Blatchley took their three boys and only girl to England. Even in parting, the youngest son, who was already sick, passed into the Promised Land. Subsequently, Mrs. Taylor fell sick and passed on painlessly to the Father at the age of thirty-three. Hudson drew ever closer to God in the painful, lonely months to come as his faith was tested.

Fifteen months later Hudson found himself returning to London and back to China again. His second wife, Miss Faulding, accompanied him as he endeavored to build up the existing work that had deteriorated terribly. Hudson would take himself to the hardest places to help straighten out difficulties and encourage the new converts and missionaries working there. He verbalized his inadequacies in a letter to his mother wherein he wrote, "Do pray earnestly for me. One more unworthy there could not be. And oh, how I feel my utter incapacity to carry out the work aright!"[54] Hudson Taylor knew the power of prayer—and had experienced it.

Then in early 1875, one of Hudson's papers on the Appeal for Prayer for China's needs made its way into the newspaper, asking for

---

54   Frederick Taylor, *Hudson Taylor and the China Inland Mission: The Growth of A Work of God* (London, China Inland Mission, 1920), 228.

missionaries to China. Missionaries began to come as God directed, and Hudson held Chinese class at his bedside due to a spinal concussion. The Lord saw these missionaries to the field, and upon arrival, they began praying for Hudson's recovery. He recovered well enough to make another journey to China with eight more missionaries as he continued his walk of faith.

China began to open up like never before and Hudson again prayed for more missionaries. The next three years were a glorious time of faith, God-answered prayers, and the stirring of peoples' hearts toward China. Not only did they get seventy new missionaries from 1882 to 1884, but in 1887 one hundred more missionaries were requested. Six hundred men and women offered themselves to the mission, of which one hundred and two were chosen. The China Inland Mission moved from an inter-denominational organization to an international one. God opened doors around the world for Hudson Taylor's message of the Chinese people. And even though the Boxer Crisis of 1900 saw the slaughter of hundreds of Christians, China opened up even further to the spread of the Gospel afterwards.

Hudson Taylor made one last trip to China, and it was there that he passed on to the other side on June 3, 1905. Without pain or suffering the Lord graciously took him home. He had the privilege of seeing the Hunan Province outreach station, which he had been burdened with for thirty years, prior to his death. And today the China Inland Mission is still in existence, known as the Overseas Missionary Fellowship; its reaches have long since gone far beyond China.

You may be saying, "Well, I'm sure not Hudson Taylor!" Undoubtedly, I can echo your sentiments. However, one of the most inspiring discoveries for me was when Hudson found how to abide in Christ and not just in his own abilities. He believed practical holiness was gradually attained by a diligent use of grace. But the more he strove after it, the more it eluded his grasp. The Lord revealed to

Hudson that what was missing was faith; yet though he strove for faith he could not attain it. He then remembered the words of his dear friend Mr. McCarthy. He said the strengthening of faith was "not by striving for faith, but by resting on the Faithful One."[55]

We "rest" on the Faithful One by coming to Him in prayer. If we could all grasp this vision, the limitations of evangelism we put on ourselves would be far less when it comes to sharing a positive spiritual comment with other people. I think about Elijah in the Old Testament and all the miracles that he did. He seemed like a man without fear most of the time. When I read about him, I think, "Boy, I'm not Elijah, God!" But the Lord reminds us all how the "effective prayer" of a person can accomplish much (James 5:16). As a matter of fact, we find out a little more about Elijah in James 5:17, when James states, "Elijah was a man with a nature like ours, and he prayed fervently that it might not rain, and for three years and six months it did not rain on the earth." God wants you and me to know that when we are led by the Holy Spirit of God, the miraculous is at our finger tips. That's why prayer is so important. It helps you discern the voice of the Holy Spirit who will lead you into places you never dreamed.

---

55 Frederick Taylor, *Hudson Taylor and the China Inland Mission*, 175.

YOUR ASSIGNMENT:
Listening To The Holy Spirit

1. Begin a devotion and prayer time in the morning if you have not already. Some people prefer the evening. But whatever works best for you, find some time that you can put on the calendar as God's time. It does not have to be long, but it should be consistent to help prayer become a part of your day.

2. During your prayer times, begin by thanking God for what He has done, then share your requests with Him, and finally take time to listen. Write down what you feel the Holy Spirit is speaking to you about—especially in the area of sharing the Gospel.

3. Begin praying about what a time of sharing with others might look like in your life. Begin praying for places and people that you might see or visit during a typical week and ask the Lord whether He wants to use you to speak in those situations.

4. When the Holy Spirit does nudge you, make sure you write down what happened so that you can look back and learn from your experiences. Rest assured, the Holy Spirit is still nudging folks today.

CHAPTER 3

LISTEN...AND EXPERIENCE
THE POWER OF PRAYER

Sitting in seat 41J, at an altitude of thirty-five thousand feet and traveling at 578 miles an hour, I suddenly had an urge to pray. Not the kind of urge that says, "it would really be nice if you prayed," or "I really need to start praying more," but the kind of urge that says "something is wrong and you must pray now!" I experienced this as I traveled to China several years ago. The realization that something was amiss was undeniable and the need for prayer imminent; but what was I to pray for? Was there something wrong with the plane; did the luggage miss the plane; or worse yet, was there a hijacker on board our flight? I did not have the answers to any of these questions, but as I began seeking God in prayer the Holy Spirit took over and I began praying "in the Spirit." The Holy Spirit began leading me to pray in a way that I did not totally understand, but with a clear conviction that I must pray until my "burden of urgency" lifted. Something was amiss and the Holy Spirit was sharing a burden of prayer with me.

> ...the Holy Spirit works in this world to lead and guide us in every aspect of our lives, to include the vital aspect of prayer.

Although I never did understand the spiritual significance of this instance, I knew, without a doubt, that God had prompted me to pray by the direction of His Holy Spirit. Without the Holy Spirit no link exists between God and mankind, except the aspect of Creator and the created. Yes, we are created in the image of God (Genesis 1:27, 9:6) and we are His children (Romans 8:16, Galatians 3:26), but it is only the Holy Spirit of God, which allows people to see themselves as such (Romans 8:16). And the Holy Spirit works in this world to lead and guide us in every aspect of our lives, including the vital aspect of prayer and the sharing of your faith with other people in your realm of influence and daily life.

While every aspect of the Holy Spirit's work is more than I could hope to cover in this chapter, I would like to focus on two main issues. The first one is the need for the Holy Spirit to help us pray, and the second is the actual role of the Holy Spirit in prayer. How does He help the believer, and non-believer for that matter, in their quest for communication with the God of the entire universe? I believe that we need the Holy Spirit of God in our prayer life more today than we have ever needed Him before, to help us in our faith conversations. In a world that seems increasingly deaf to the Christian call, only Spirit-empowered prayer will make a difference in our lives, our outreach efforts, and our faith conversations.

WHY DO WE NEED THE HOLY SPIRIT TO PRAY?

To say that the Holy Spirit is important in our everyday life is like saying we must have water to survive. As a matter of fact, without the Holy Spirit, salvation itself would not even be possible. Even the Apostle Paul clearly reveals to us that "finite man's search for

45

God is his fundamental characteristic, given to him by God"[56] and a characteristic in which the Holy Spirit plays a crucial role. There is no question that without the Holy Spirit we would be forever blinded by sin to our true fallen state. And as Christians, we can empathize with the Apostle Paul that the battle against sin never ceases, as he shares in Romans chapter seven. It is this sin, which has left man "indisposed to pray as he should, for it has also blinded him to his real needs."[57] So we often pray selfishly, led by our emotions, desiring only to fulfill our own lusts—sadly, without a real faith that God would answer our petitions anyway.

We need not explore our society very far to see that sin has left us in a crisis situation, in which the Church appears to have fallen asleep. According to The Barna Group, in a poll dated December 17, 2001, "at least three out of ten born again adults say that co-habitation, gay sex, sexual fantasies, breaking the speed limit, or watching sexually-explicit movies are morally acceptable behaviors."[58] While some may argue for the irrelevance of this data as time passes, a more recent statistic confirms surprising commonalities between the churched and churchless:

> Churchless people tend to live a somewhat 'edgier' life—they are more likely to use profanity, get drunk, or view immodest images via the media. But their social interactions—their conversations about faith and morals, and the likelihood of

---

56 Hans Urs Von Balthasar, "Prayer," *Cummunio: International Catholic Review* (Fall 1985): 246.

57 Robert F. Boyd, "The Work of the Holy Spirit in Prayer: An Exposition of Romans 8:26, 27," *Interpretation: A Journal of Bible and Theology* 8 (January 1954): 39.

58 Barna Research, Ltd., "The Year's Most Intriguing Findings, From Barna Research Studies," [publication online]; available from http://www.barna.org; Internet; accessed 26 March 2002.

their engaging in behaviors such as gossip, lying, or sexual activity outside of marriage—are all but indistinguishable from churchgoers.[59]

Barna notes that a significant percentage of those attending church services have not even accepted Jesus Christ as Lord and Savior, mainly due to the lack of conviction and power in the Church today—the conviction and power that only comes from the Holy Spirit of God and a congregation dedicated to prayer.

Sadly, the facts do not halt there. Even in America's own "born again" community, in April of 1997, 52% of born again Christians denied "Satan's existence" and 55% rejected "the existence of the Holy Spirit."[60] Although the number rejecting the Holy Spirit fell three percentage points to 52% in 2001, the Church faces an epidemic, wherein the life-giving source of the Holy Spirit is being slowly cut off. In a Barna report on April 13, 2009, they stated: "Overall, 38% strongly agreed and 20% agreed somewhat that the Holy Spirit is 'a symbol of God's power or presence but is not a living entity.'"[61] This epidemic has even impacted our commitment to having faith conversations. "In 1993, nine out of 10 Christians agreed that 'every Christian has a responsibility to share their faith' (89%). Today (2018), just two-thirds say so (64%)…a 25-point drop."[62] These statistics reveal that the state of most Christians'

---

59 George Barna and David Kinnaman, *Churchless: Understanding Today's Unchurched and How to Connect with Them* (Carol Stream, IL: Tyndale, 2014), 132.

60 Barna Research, Ltd., "Angels Are In – Devils & Holy Spirit Are Out," [publication online]; available from http://www.barna.org; Internet; accessed 26 March 2002.

61 Barna Research, Ltd., "Most American Christians Do Not Believe that Satan or the Holy Spirit Exist," [publication online]; available from http://www.barna.org; Internet; accessed 3 March 2019.

62 The Barna Group, *Spiritual Conversations In The Digital Age*, ebook (2018), 12.

relationship with their heavenly Father, His Holy Spirit, and His Son are deteriorating. Honestly, when any relationship becomes distant, you tend to disregard what is important in that relationship—whether spiritual or physical. And that distance only increases when prayer is absent.

Even as Christians, we sometimes become more consumed with appearances and technological advancements than taking time to nurture a right relationship with God. With everyone carrying planners, notebooks, and smart phones, every minute of our lives necessitates scheduling. It appears that now, "we live to perform rather than to be."[63] Social media has only heightened the need to perform. But have we in the Church become so professional that we no longer remember how to just sit in the presence of a loving, holy God and experience the immensity of His great love and forgiveness, through the time-tested avenue of prayer? I don't think so, but it's a battle to make time for God. I'm the world's worst at doing things backwards!

> I have to remind myself on a continual basis that God comes first—my most important events of the day and everything else can wait.

When I get up in the morning, I just want to have my coffee and start checking email, social media, the latest news, and THEN read my Bible and talk to God. I have to remind myself on a continual basis that God comes first—my most important events of the day and everything else can wait. After all—prayer should be my "most important event," shouldn't it?

It is a sad reality that "sin leaves the will of a man damaged, and his perception of spiritual truths and needs is seriously

---

63   Robert L. Brandt and Zenas J. Bicket, "The Spirit Helps Us Pray: A Biblical Theology of Prayer," (Springfield: Logon Press, 1973): 19.

handicapped,"[64] but what a comfort to know that God Himself helps us in our prayers to Him! God loves His children so much He even helps them pray in order that He may answer those prayers; all the while using those petitions as vehicles to ever increase our faith, through the leading and teaching of the Holy Spirit. There is no doubt a spiritual link exists between the believer and the One whom he or she can call "Father." We must strive to be vessels of honor for the Spirit's use. As 1 Corinthians 6:20 (KJV) states: "For ye are bought with a price: therefore glorify God in your body, and in your spirit, which are God's."[65]

The path from sin to salvation is a life-transforming experience. It is only through the work of the Holy Spirit that we are adopted into God's family, gaining a place of sonship (a biblical term designating position not a gender), as well as becoming joint-heirs with Christ. Thus, we have the extreme privilege of coming to God as a son or daughter to a father, whereby we can cry, "Abba Father," in our times of worship and prayer. How vivid the picture becomes as Jesus tells us the story concerning the love of a father for a son, and how much more our heavenly Father gives us those "good gifts" requested of Him in Matthew chapter seven. The Apostle Paul even told us in 1 Corinthians 2:14a, "The man without the Spirit does not accept the things that come from the Spirit of God," revealing our desperate need for the Holy Spirit.

Paul also reveals the interaction that the believer should have with the Holy Spirit in 2 Corinthians 13:14, "May the grace of the Lord Jesus Christ, and the love of God, and the fellowship of the Holy Spirit be with you all." We are to have "fellowship" with the Holy Spirit, the third person of the Holy Trinity! It is this fellowship

---

64 Robert F. Boyd, 41.

65 All Scripture references will be from, *The English Standard Bible*, (Wheaton, IL: Crossway) 2001, unless noted otherwise.

that allows the believer to know God in greater measure and grow in spiritual strength. Paul tells us in Ephesians 3:16, "I pray that out of his glorious riches he may strengthen you with power through his Spirit in your inner being." The Holy Spirit has initiated our fellowship with the Father, Son, and Holy Spirit through His work of "contrition" in our lives during the salvation process. This is that godly sorrow, which brings one to the point of repentance of sins and confession of Jesus Christ as Lord and Savior of their life.

But why is it that some people within the Church feel uncomfortable entering into an intimate relationship with God? Could it be that the "spirit of the age" has found a way into the Church? A great friend who has passed on to his heavenly home, Reverend Ron Auch, talked about the parallel relationship of a man and woman in marriage and Jesus's relationship, as the bridegroom, to the Church (believers), which is the "bride of Christ." He said that Jesus "never determines the degree of intimacy he will have with the church," but that "the final decision is always the prerogative of the Church."[66] And just as the Church can resist intimacy with the Son, so the Church can "quench" the Holy Spirit of God and refuse His invitation or leading. If this were not possible, why would Paul admonish those in Thessalonica, and us today, to "quench not the Spirit" (1 Thessalonians 5:19)?

There is an adversary that we can contend with only in prayer, because, Paul tells us in 2 Corinthians 10:3, even though we walk "in the flesh," our "war" is not "after the flesh." Paul continues in verse 4: "the weapons we fight with are not the weapons of the world." We must fight our battles of spiritual warfare with the weapon of Spirit-empowered prayer and God's Word because "the enemy of

---

66   Ron Auch, "Prayer Can Change Your Marriage," (Green Forest: New Leaf, 1984): 43.

the soul knows the power of prayer."[67] Prayer is one of the keys to building up our immunity to the wiles of the Devil and gaining precious ground in the spiritual realm. The well-known minister and graduate of Yale divinity school, R.A. Torrey, once said, "The price of a revival is honest, earnest prayer in the Holy Spirit, prayer that will not take no for an answer."[68] Rees Howells, fully believed that, "Only the Holy Spirit himself can lead the intercessor into that realm where the basic conflict between God and the enemy actually operates,"[69] and then hold the intercessor liable—through an almost palpable burden to pray—until the spiritual battle is over and the burden lifted.

The Holy Spirit is vital to the believer in the area of spiritual warfare and sharing his or her faith, because only the Holy Spirit of God can direct us to pray effectively in this battle for ourselves, our loved ones, and those God will bring into our lives. It is only by prayer and the diligent study of God's Word that "the Spirit gives wisdom to demolish"[70] every weapon of the enemy. It is only the Holy Spirit that keeps us vibrant and hungry for the things of God. Without the Holy Spirit we will fall prey to the Devil's lies. Prayer is the "oxygen" that keeps the spiritual fires burning brightly and aids us in overcoming the darkness that pervades this world. Jesus even told us in Mark 14:38, "the spirit is willing but the body is weak," and He admonishes us to pray in earnest so that we will not become ensnared by the temptations of the Devil.

---

67   Thomas E. Trask and Wayde I. Goodall, "The Battle," (Grand Rapids: Zondervan, 1997): 133.

68   R.A. Torrey, "The Fundamentals: A Testimony to the Truth," Vol 3, *The AGES Digital Library* (Albany: AGES Software, 1997): 191.

69   Doris M. Ruscoe, "The Intercession of Rees Howells," (Cambridge: Lutterworth Press, 1983): 54.

70   Robert L. Brandt and Zenas J. Bicket, 277.

One final reason supporting the need for the Holy Spirit in prayer is that we must worship God "in spirit," and it is the Holy Spirit who has drawn us unto the Father, and only the Holy Spirit knows the mind of God. The Apostle Paul reminds us in 1 Corinthians 2:11, "For who among men knows the thoughts of a man except the man's spirit within him? In the same way no one knows the thoughts of God except the Spirit of God." John 4:24 states, "God is spirit, and those who worship Him must worship in spirit and truth." Truly, we need the Holy Spirit more today than we have ever needed Him before, in order to pray in harmony with the mind of God and hear the Holy Spirit's voice when He guides us.

THE ROLE OF THE HOLY SPIRIT IN PRAYER

The initial role of the Holy Spirit is one allowing Him to be the "Spirit of the dialogue"[71] between humanity and the Father and Son. As children of God we can freely choose to come before Him (Galatians 5:13), seeking His will for our lives through our prayers and petitions. Romans 8:15 and Galatians 4:6 reveal a spiritual link between the believer and God, provided by the Holy Spirit, through confession on the part of humanity. In the early Church, "the reception of the Spirit and the act of baptism were intimately connected,"[72] and only after baptism could believers call God, "Father."

We need to realize though, that asking according to the will of God (1 John 5:14) can be about anything from your son's baseball game to the salvation of the lost, when led by the Holy Spirit. Who are we to say what is or is not the will of God? Have we grown so

---

71   Robert F. Boyd, 251.

72   E.A. Obeng, "Abba Father: The Prayer of the Sons of God," *The Expository Times* 99 (Summer 1988): 365.

mightily in our endeavors for spiritual excellence that we can rightly judge the correctness of every prayer? I think not. Truly God uses the foolish things of this world to confound the wise (1 Corinthians 1:27) and the innocence of children to halt the pride of life. May we strive for sensitivity in the Spirit, in order that we might encourage those desiring to walk in the Spirit of a gracious and just God.

Another role of the Holy Spirit is that of spiritual guide. There is no question that "prayer is our primary pathway of relationship to God,"[73] and the only guide able to lead us on the right spiritual path is the Holy Spirit. The Apostle Paul writes that there are times when the Holy Spirit prays "in us" and "sometimes that it is we who pray in the Spirit,"[74] indicating that the Holy Spirit works jointly with our own spirit. It is the Holy Spirit who leads us to confession, guides us in our petitions, and moves upon us to intercede for others, turning our fleshly bodies into temples for the purpose of carrying out God's own desires by giving us His desires. Rees Howells shares about this aspect of the Holy Spirit by telling us, "I hadn't the faintest idea of the love of the Holy Ghost for a lost soul, until He loved one through me."[75] It is the Holy Spirit who guides us in prayer and enables us to pray with determination and fervor. Truly, the real assurance of the Holy Spirit's role in prayer is "the harmony of our prayer with the mind of God."[76] It is this harmony that helps us see opportunities for sharing our faith with others.

---

73 Siang-Tan and Douglas H. Gregg, "Disciplines of the Holy Spirit: How to Connect to the Spirit's Power and Presence," (Grand Rapids: Zondervan, 1997): 66.

74 E.A. Obeng, 365.

75 Siang-Tan and Douglas H. Gregg, 201.

76 H.F. Woodhouse, "Pneumatology and Prayer," *Studia Liturgica* 5 no.1 (Spring 1966): 57.

Another major role of the Holy Spirit revolves around intercession and our need for help in life's struggles, which can be seen in Romans 8:26-27. We see that,

> In the same way, the Spirit helps us in our weakness. We do not know what we ought to pray for, but the Spirit himself intercedes for us with groans that words cannot express. And he who searches our hearts knows the mind of the Spirit, because the Spirit intercedes for the saints in accordance with God's will.

Paul reveals that the Spirit is helping us even "in our weakness." We think we know how to pray; however, as James 4:3 tells us, we have a great tendency to pray "according to our passions." But here we see that the Holy Spirit intercedes with "groans" that cannot be expressed with mere words. Groans that only God the Father, the Son, and the Holy Spirit can understand, because God alone, as Jeremiah 17:10 states, is the One who searches the hearts and knows our thoughts.

In Romans 8:26, the Revised Standard Version states that the intercession of the Spirit for us includes "sighs too deep for words." It is this multi-faceted role of the Holy Spirit in prayer that reveals His importance and demands His presence. Only through the intimate vehicle of prayer are we able to nurture and strengthen this relationship with the Holy Spirit and our heavenly Father. This was a foreign thought in early Jewish life according to Craig Keener: "Judaism usually viewed the Spirit as an expression of God's power rather than as a personal being; like John (chapters 14-16), Paul views the Spirit as a personal being (cf. 2 Corinthians 13:14),"[77]

---

77   Craig S. Keener, *The IVP Bible Background Commentary*, 2nd ed. (Downers Grove, IL:2014), 441.

confirming the personal role that the Holy Spirit has in every believer's life. This role is further confirmed in Romans 8:38-39, where the Apostle Paul shows us that nothing "can separate us from the love of God that is in Christ Jesus our Lord." It is this same love that reaches out to us in the person of the Holy Spirit and compels us to share the goodness of God with others.

Paul states in Romans 8:34 that Jesus is at the right hand of the Father "interceding" for us, and in Romans 8:26, we see that the Holy Spirit of God is interceding for us here on earth. There may even be times when the divine so interacts with us that we cannot distinguish who is praying, whether we are praying through the Holy Spirit, or the Holy Spirit is praying through us. But undoubtedly, without the leading of the Holy Spirit we are handicapped and unable to pray with certainty of God's divine will. As 1 Corinthians 2:9-10 discloses, God has revealed His purposes to the believer "by His Spirit," and that it is the Spirit of God who "searches all things, even the deep things of God." When we say the Holy Spirit "searches" the things of God we must realize that "searches does not suggest incompleteness, but rather the opposite—fullness of knowledge, action, and penetration."[78]

It is interesting to note that the Greek word *sunantilambanetai* (yes, it's as hard to say as it looks) that is found in Romans 8:26 is a form of the word *sunantilambanomai* and is translated as the "spirit helps us." This same verb form is found in four other instances in the Scriptures, with the first in Exodus 18:22, where Moses' father-in-law is revealing the need for "judges" that will help "bear the burden with you" (NAS). In Numbers 11:17, we see that God is preparing to commission the seventy elders, and He tells Moses that they "shall bear the burden of the people with you." Psalm 89:21

---

78   Paul A. Hamar, "The Book of First Corinthians," (Springfield: Gospel Publishing House, 1980): 27.

reveals that God Himself "will sustain" His servant David, and in Luke 10:40 we see Martha's frustration with her sister Mary, who has chosen to sit at the feet of Jesus while Martha works in the kitchen. In every instance, we see this word used in the sense of helping to carry or sustain, conveying the reassurance that the Holy Spirit's intercession is helping us. It is not so important whether the Holy Spirit is sustaining or bearing burdens; what is important is the realization that you are not alone in the fight.

It is also interesting to see that the role of intercession is noted, in Romans 8:26, with the Greek word *huperentugchanei*, which is a form of the word *huperentugchano* (another stomach-churning pronunciation). This word, with the prefix *huper*, is only used here, and is used without the prefix in the very next verse. In almost every instance where a word is compounded like this, "the words carry the added idea of 'above measure,' or 'to a higher degree,'"[79] implying that the Holy Spirit prays and intercedes in and through us, above our own abilities. This confirms that there is really only one "master" of intercession, and that is the Holy Spirit.

But there is another realm of spiritual activity with regard to believers, and that is praying in the spirit, according to Jude 20: "But you, dear friends, build yourselves up in your most holy faith and pray in the Holy Spirit." Additionally, we see in Acts 2:4 that "praying in tongues is made possible by the enablement of the Holy Spirit."[80] Praying in the spirit is surely praying that emerges from within the believer—the temple of the Holy Spirit. Paul admonishes us to "pray in the Spirit on all occasions, with all kinds of prayers and requests," in Ephesians 6:18, and truly it is only "in the Spirit" that genuine prayer can permeate the spiritual realm of this physical life. Prayer must be Spirit-breathed. The Holy Spirit

---

79   Robert F. Boyd, 38.

80   Robert L. Brandt and Zenas J. Bicket, 28.

alone leads us to repentance, reveals imminent needs, and moves us to intercession—all while praying through us, whether in one's heavenly prayer language of tongues—called glossolalia—or your own native language.

A last role of the Holy Spirit is that of teacher and illuminator. It is interesting that the Spirit of God never tries to magnify Himself. He has been sent to glorify God and testify of the Lord Jesus Christ, being his "witness" (John 15:26), and who teaches us all things (John 14:26). The Holy Spirit will only convey what he is supposed to (John 16:13-15), striving not to lead us into a greater knowledge of Himself per se, but to a greater knowledge of Jesus Christ. In talking about our faith journey with others, it is this role of illumination that may prompt you to ask certain questions or share certain portions of your testimony or some other personal experience you may have encountered. A special Scripture may even come to mind that the Lord prompts you to share, opening surprising doors for faith conversations.

It is the Spirit of God who inspired the writing of Scripture (2 Timothy 3:16), and it is the same Spirit, preserving Scripture and quickening the Word of God within us, bringing the Scriptures to life. It is the Spirit of God who caused Jeremiah to declare that God's Word was "a fire shut up in my bones," as he prayed to God (Jeremiah 20:9). And it is the Spirit of God—through prayer—who stirs up the Scriptures, written on our hearts, giving us strength for the battles, compassion for the suffering, and unceasing love for the unlovable. "It is not that we pray, but he that prays in us;"[81] and this same Spirit, not only gave us the faith to believe unto salvation, but has also spoken by God's chosen servants to His people since time began.

---

81 S.G. Hall, "The Prayer of the Church. What We Ask and How We Ask It," *The Expository Times* 96 (December 1984): 73.

SUMMARY

The great intercessor Rees Howells shared that having the Holy Spirit was like living in a whole new realm, which helps transform our minds in Christ, according to Romans 12:2. It is only through the Holy Spirit that we are able to declare and share our faith in God (1 Corinthians 12:4), while praying with assurance. It is this act of prayer, which is the "invocation of God," that lets us enter into a place of fellowship with God. Prayer frees us from the thoughts and hindrances of this world, in order to bask in the overwhelming love, peace and fellowship of God. It is the Christian's prayer life, which maintains the spiritual lifeline to God, and if prayer maintains a lifeline, then lack of prayer reflects a malnourished believer, Church, and ultimately, world.

The Holy Spirit actively works in our life of prayer, helping us attain a greater intimacy with God and providing a means of spiritual nourishment that empowers us to be witnesses for Christ. One of the most important aspects of salvation is having a "relationship" with a living God who cares for us; and you cannot nurture a relationship without spending time working on that relationship. If someone is married, he or she did not just drive up and ask his or her spouse the marriage question! There was a period of courtship, where thoughts and dreams were shared while getting to know each other. God has a similar desire to know His Church, and He holds out His hand of courtship to every single one of His children.

Today when we hear the loud prayers of those in our midst, may it remind us that "prayer is not chatter with God, but speaking with him as friend to friend."[82] This speaking should also include a sizeable amount of listening. It is the Spirit of God who helps us

---

82   Georges Chantraine, "Prayer Within the Church," *Communio: International Catholic Review* 12 (Fall 1985): 262.

along this journey with our heavenly Father, a journey that leads us into greater intimacy with God and an intimacy that helps us know God's heart—through prayer. Intimacy has been a word marred and exploited by the world, becoming a word that Christians are even ashamed to use. But my prayer is that every Christian might see spiritual intimacy today as the ultimate pursuit of every prayer, attainable only through the leading of God's Holy Spirit.

CHAPTER 4

ENGAGE

L.E.A.R.N. Evangelism means to:

ENGAGE – You must decide to engage another person in conversation.

Oftentimes people stumble with engagement because today's culture teaches us to respect other people's privacy and to embrace tolerance. Additionally, many Christians lean toward a more introverted personality, so engaging others is a challenge for them. Rebecca Pippert shared a timeless truth in her classic book, *Out of the Saltshaker and into the World*: "Being an extrovert isn't essential to evangelism—obedience and love are."[83] You may be the person who prefers engaging others via a handwritten note or sending web page links to articles or blog posts that mean a lot to you. Regardless of your preferred method, God can use that to speak to others.

However, there is no better means of communication than actually talking to someone. For Christians who are extroverts, this is an exciting opportunity because they have never met a stranger— ever! Pray for God's peace and courage as you step out in obedience

---

83 Rebecca Manley Pippert, 123.

to His Word (Mark 16:15). Try starting mini-conversations with people about the weather, aspects of their jobs, or honest compliments for service. These can start conversations where you end up talking about God's greatest gift. In the following pages I'll share a few engaging opportunities that might help you as you step out to engage others.

Easy Evangelism

While on a trip with my family to the East Coast, I had an interesting evangelistic encounter. Now, I'm not an in-your-face evangelist spewing out Bible mandates and condemnations. And even though I love to preach and share biblical insights into Scripture, sharing my faith through one-on-one relational evangelism is something I really enjoy. I like the opportunity to familiarize myself with folks and listen to what might be going on in their lives. Then, whenever the Lord seems to prompt me with those little urgings that could be described as more intuition than a literal voice booming out of the shadows, I drop a word here or there. Perhaps a question to ponder, not necessarily a spiritual question, but a question that lets a person verbalize what their particular path might look like a little farther down the road.

A case in point happened on our flight to Newport News, Virginia. I happened to sit in the aisle seat across from my family with an open seat beside me. As we settled in on the last leg of our trip from Atlanta to Newport News, Sherry[84] happened to be one of the last passengers to board. Since it was a packed flight, she sat next to me. Sherry was very talkative and worked in insurance, so our conversation took off. Since she hated flying and was extremely nervous about it all, she

---

84 Not her real name.

did most of the talking. She said it was ironic that she hated flying because with her recent promotion she had to fly frequently. She had never married and talked about how she would one day love to have someone with whom to spend her life.

Sherry led the conversation to life issues and disclosed that she had just bought her first brand new Lexus. I love anything with an engine, so that helped propel us into further dialog. She was going to visit her mom in North Carolina, and when she found out that I was a minister, she said "I knew there was a good spirit about you." I enjoyed the compliment since those don't always happen, but it allowed us to talk about other spiritual matters as the conversation progressed. I mainly asked questions and she did most of the talking.

Sherry talked as though she had been in church her whole life, but when we started talking about community involvement and helping others less fortunate, she confessed that she did not attend church like she had in the past. She shared that she used to be very involved in providing meals to the disabled, but when she finally bought a new house and moved, the opportunity to continue that part of her life was across town and not really feasible anymore.

As we talked about giving to the community and how much Sherry had to offer, I encouraged her to try to find a church that met her needs. I stated that perhaps she needed a smaller church that was family oriented. She acknowledged how she missed being a part of a local congregation and said that she needed to get back in church and closer to God. I shared how God just really wanted her to know how much He loved her and wanted to show that love to her. I told Sherry that a healthy community of faith welcomes people and gives them opportunities to express themselves and sense God's presence in a safe environment.

All this time I had not really initiated that much about spiritual issues or God. The conversation just went there by itself, and I prayed that the Lord would help me encourage Sherry and bring to my mind the right words to say and questions to ask.

When we were talking about marriage and relationships, Sherry shared that she had a gentleman she was dating and that he had a couple of children from a previous marriage. She also had shared that her mom had raised her since her dad had left when she was young. I was able to share how whenever people enter into a relationship, it has the tendency to become physical. When physical relationships happen there is a deeper bonding that takes place, and sometimes we mistake that feeling as a completeness to something else that is lacking in our lives. I talked about how difficult it is to not get physical when dating and becoming close to someone, but then when it did get physical, we often allow that temporal feeling to placate our deeper needs.

It was a great conversation, and I felt as though God had allowed me to have this conversation with Sherry to encourage not only her, but also myself. Even talking about the physical aspects of relationships seemed like such a God-directed initiative, because that is definitely not something I would normally initiate with someone I don't know!

I share all this merely as an example that "closing the deal" alone does not constitute proper evangelism protocol. Every Christian should continually work at being a Christian, and part of that entails conversing with others. As Christians, we should look for avenues to help others, or otherwise display our "Christianity." How Christian are you? Do you pray for opportunities? Do you look for opportunities? God will bring those opportunities if we will but ask—and listen.

Another evangelism opportunity presented itself when checking out of our hotel. I usually carry some specialty witnessing brochures. They're not really Gospel tracts per se, but small pamphlets that cost about $1 each or less—you might even get a volume discount. I don't throw them around everywhere but try to have one or two available with me when I travel, or have a couple in my vehicle in case a special opportunity presents itself.

The particular booklet I had with me was entitled *Discover How To Choose Your Faith Path* by Mark Mittelberg. I put a five-dollar bill inside the booklet and left it on the dresser. It is normal to tip the hotel staff who clean your room, and especially so after several days, so I tried to accomplish two things at once. You might say, "But what if they just throw it away?" Well, I always pray and ask God to bless the material and the person who might pick it up. I can never feel responsible for someone else's decision, but I can enhance people's opportunities for exposure to the Gospel.

I have long believed that God is big enough to prove Himself if given the chance. I also think that Jesus can speak louder and clearer than I can if folks will just read the Scriptures for themselves. Obviously, as a minister, I appreciate preaching ministries and all the various other ministries that strive to show God's love and grace. But I know that I can never make someone else believe in Jesus Christ; I can only present these truths in appealing ways that encourage others to take a look at Jesus in their own private way.

People often want to discover answers to important questions by themselves. When we allow people room to wrestle with the greatest question of life, we give God room to work more effectively in that person's life. Too often we force our cultural preferences and societal norms on others of similar, and very dissimilar, cultures. People process material in somewhat similar ways, but oftentimes the decision-making process can range from very individualist to family oriented. In an Asian context, decisions are often made as a family unit and it is not uncommon to see whole families make decisions to follow Christ at one time. Thus, allowing opportunities for other people to explore and experiment with the Jesus of Nazareth seems crucial.

All that aside, leaving a less than one-dollar booklet behind that could possibly be thrown away seems like a small price to pay for potentially making an eternal difference in a person's life. This is also a great way for Christians who loathe confrontational witness to evangelize in a way that is no less meaningful to the one who picks up and reads that Christian booklet. How many stories have Christians read about individuals who picked up a Gideon Bible in a hotel room and found Christ? Every Gideon and person who contributed financially toward getting those Bibles in those hotels will share in the celebration of that new believer—whether here on earth or when we finally reach our heavenly home.

I also like to take some devotional booklets with me at times, like Max Lucado's 40-day devotional called *Trust More Fear Less*. When prompted by the Holy Spirit, I will usually share these with friends or acquaintances. I might hand them a copy and say something light like, "Hey, I thought you might enjoy a little bathroom reader." In doing this, I'm respecting my acquaintances' privacy and spiritual preferences, yet I'm showing how much I care by giving them a little something that is written by a popular author and can be perused at their leisure. It doesn't look all that spiritual and the title seems appealing.

Sometimes, I like to do random acts of kindness that may bless others who normally serve us—just like the unsuspecting pastor's wife who received a nice surprise one evening. My family voted to go to a local establishment for ice cream. We happened to notice quite a few folks ahead of us, who then moved into a special meeting room. One of the ladies who had been with the group was actually behind us as we ordered our ice cream. We struck up a casual conversation, and when we got to the cashier, I told the worker that I wanted to purchase the ice cream for the lady standing behind us. The lady behind us asked, "Are you serious? Why would you do that?" I told her that we just wanted to show God's love in practical ways. After I paid, the lady asked who I was, and she introduced herself as the wife of a local pastor I knew. As a matter of fact, she was the pastor's wife of one of the largest churches in town! She said that she really appreciated the ice cream and nice gesture because she had endured a really rough week. While we sat and ate our ice cream the pastor actually came over and thanked us as well.

Just like unbelievers, Christians need the Gospel, the good news, which is what happens when evangelism takes place. So, go evangelize! Ask God for opportunities that fit your personality and your comfort level (or the comfort level He knows you can handle), and then begin scattering seed like there is no tomorrow. You'll be amazed at the unexpected divine appointments God will provide for you to share the good news and encourage others.

Evangelism In The Workplace

If you are a business owner, and especially if retail stores are in your bundle of challenges you have to wrestle with every day, evangelism can be as easy as having one or two nice evangelistic pamphlets for your potential customers. Don't litter your counter with cheap witnessing tracts that focus more on hell than heaven. You want to refrain from leaving the reader beaten up instead of lifted up when they come to your place of business. If you don't, they will surely remember your business—but for the wrong reason!

Evangelism doesn't have to involve metaphorically shoving a Bible down someone's throat or putting yet another fake million-dollar bill as a tip on a table. As a matter of fact, if you love handing out tracts and leaving them on tables after you're served, I pray that you at least leave a gracious tip (20% or more) along with that track. Tip in a manner that is consistent for your area—the point is to be an unexpected blessing! If your livelihood depended on customer tips, would you appreciate getting a fake bill with no tip? I seriously doubt it!

Everyone appreciates quality materials. Whether you operate a welding shop or finer fashions, small evangelistic pamphlets allow customers to quickly "browse" while they're in the checkout line.

Setting out a small number of these booklets allows customers the opportunity to pick one up for free (yes, they should be free) without being too conspicuous. Business owners in the retail book business will obviously have a slightly different approach, because their sheer volume of traffic could put them out of business if every customer took a nice evangelistic pamphlet like, "Imagine Your Life Without Fear" by Max Lucado or "Your Faith Path" by Mark Mittelberg, just to name a couple.

The object is to pick out something that rings true with you and make sure you have read whatever you put out! Nice pamphlets like the ones mentioned above can easily be a part of businesses like dentists' and doctors' offices (if it is your own private practice), on checkout counters of regular retail businesses (again if it is your own business), or any number of other places. You could even have a special kiosk of sorts for your front door or some other strategic location within your store if so desired.

All the while, you have not confronted one single person about Christianity, hell or heaven, the crucifixion, or even how you got radically "saved" (a word that most non-church people don't understand). You are just going about your business and "minding the store." You have provided safe (no one's looking) opportunities for other non-churched, or even previously-churched individuals to explore the Christian faith and what it might look like in their lives. They have been given the opportunity to pick up a copy of evangelistic material at the front counter or a strategic location in your place of business—even by the door so they can get one on their way out! Congratulations! You are now doing evangelism and you didn't have to say a word!

Some Christians I know keep a devotional book on their desk, out of the way so it does not interfere with work. Speaking of not interfering with work, never take advantage of your employer's time. By that I mean that Christians should set the example in their work ethic, so giving short answers to faith questions is appropriate. When you place a faith-oriented resource in plain sight, it will hopefully raise questions for you. Short answers are great because you are busy! However, if longer conversations are needed, schedule a time that does not conflict with work responsibilities. A Christian works to represent Christ in every aspect of his or her life—including the workplace.

Learning How To Dance

When I first went to college the craze was country dancing. Spending a lot of growing-up years in the country did not allow for much time going to dances and such since there was always a lot of work to be done. But the dances that I was able to attend seemed to focus more on just moving around a bit and not really worrying too much about your style on the dance floor. The less attention you drew to yourself the better!

This was not the case upon entering college. Country-style dancing demanded a knowledge of the differing styles of dance steps, including: the two-step, polka, and line dancing moves like the 10-step, Schottische, or Cotton-Eyed Joe. I can't tell you how apprehensive I was the first time I got out on the dance floor with someone I wanted to dance with. First, I went with friends and they begin to show me how to dance with some of the easier steps. Then, I got a little braver as my familiarity grew. I really enjoyed dancing when I was younger, so dancing seemed to be a nice outlet for my friends and me. I wasn't all that close to the Lord back in those days, and I know folks have differing views on dancing, but bear with me for a bit as I try to share some relevant truths that might help you with faith conversations.

In any activity where you need to work with other people (like a dance partner), you will likely encounter various dispositions anywhere from nice to nasty as you step out on the dance floor of life. I can't tell you how many times I faltered myself—missing my steps or stepping on a foot—ouch! But I just tried my best to be gracious and apologetic when I messed up, which most folks thankfully accepted.

Why in the world am I sharing about dancing? Well, I think we can learn some great lessons about evangelism and talking about our faith journey from dancing experiences. When you begin your dancing debut, you are awkward and mechanical. You are making the right movements, but they are usually without feeling because you are trying to concentrate! Have you ever tried to thread a needle? It takes concentration—not to mention a good set of eyes. But after you have been dancing for years, it all becomes natural and flows like a cool gentle breeze in summer—you don't even have to think about it.

The same can be said about the first time you tied your own shoe, or the first time you did your own load of laundry. The very first time you changed a diaper, helped a cow give birth to a calf, rode the subway, cooked a turkey, made chocolate chip cookies, or drove in a big city. Whenever we do something for the very first time there is a bit of anxiety, and when we do it with another person there is the added uncertainty of how they will respond. The same is true whenever you take a huge chance and share something as personal as your faith. It's so personal that it stings when your efforts are rejected. But, oftentimes, the obviousness of our discomfort opens the door to receptivity by the person God is nudging us to talk to about Him.

Over the years, I have had the opportunity to read some wonderful books on sharing one's faith that helped me realize the immense value of encouragement. But, I've also read some authors who seem to condemn a reader or criticize folks for what they have not done. I do believe the Scriptures are clear (Matthew 28:19) that we have a mandate from God to share our faith with others who do not know Jesus Christ. Some people obviously have a special gift for this. Evangelist Luis Palau concurs: "Evangelism is a matter of obedience. Every Christian is called to witness. But some of us have the gift of evangelism. The main difference is that evangelists have a special push to win souls—a special desire to do something more than just witnessing during the course of everyday life."[85] But I also believe there is a learning curve to sharing our faith and that we often need more encouragement than criticism. Having a support system of fellow believers, family, and friends that will encourage you can be a tremendous asset when it comes to stepping out in obedience to God's commands. So be encouraged—you're a natural! How do I know that? Because you are a child of God and He doesn't make mistakes.

The value of encouragement became apparent in my own life when I was going through Ranger training at a military summer basic boot camp (no, not THE Ranger school; this was just a ranger segment during our basic military training). We were challenged to climb a 25-foot ladder, then walk about 25 feet on a 12-inch-wide plank to another ladder where we climbed another 15 feet to a rope that we crawled out on before dropping into the water 40 feet below. The interesting thing about this obstacle is that the 12-inch-wide plank had a large block of wood about three-fourths of the way across that we had to step over.

You may be thinking, "Well, that's not bad!" However, the rope handles that were on the first half of the plank walkway suddenly disappeared! There was nothing to hold on to when we crossed that final section of our wooden plank where the block of wood was waiting for us. On top of that, I noticed that every time someone dropped from the rope into the water below, the framework of the entire obstacle would sway back and forth—nice! So, you had to

---

85   Luis Palau and Timothy Robnett, *Telling the Story: Evangelism for the Next Generation* (Ventura, CA: Regal, 2006). 130.

pick the right time when you let go of those rope handles and walk across that plank. As our buddies made their way across the obstacle one at a time, not one time did someone say a negative comment like: "Go ahead and quit. You won't make it anyway!" Just the opposite happened. During our training, our unit became a tight-knit group and encouraged each other throughout the entire course of training. Every person was cheering everyone on to the final goal.

Can I tell you something? God and all His saints are cheering you on. The Apostle Paul shared some profound advice with the Philippian church in Philippians 3:13-14.

> *Brothers, I do not consider that I have made it my own. But one thing I do: forgetting what lies behind and straining forward to what lies ahead, I press on toward the goal for the prize of the upward call of God in Christ Jesus.*

There is a prize for every follower of Jesus Christ, and that is one of the reasons that we nail our anxieties on the Cross and speak that timely word in season (Proverbs 15:23). Engaging another person with some encouragement about your own faith journey may just be a very special prize for someone who is struggling and ready to end it all. I want to encourage you today. Even though you may feel that you are not very good at sharing anything with anyone, take a step of faith—and begin to dance like there's no tomorrow.

YOUR ASSIGNMENT:
Reflection, Sharing, And Application

1. If you are in a group setting, share one fear that you would like the Lord to help you overcome that others can help you pray about. When by yourself, write down your request in your own prayer journal and seek the Lord for victory over that fear.

2. Ask the Lord for specific opportunities to share the hope that is within you or what God has done in your life this week.

3. Pray for specific people that you encounter on a regular basis at work, at the grocery store, at the bank, at school, or any other specific people or places that the Lord puts on your heart.

4. Make a list of two or three quality faith pamphlets that you could display somewhere if you are a business owner, or one nice pamphlet or devotion book that you could set out of the way on your desk at work. These little visible resources raise questions that can lead to fruitful conversations.

5. When you are at work (or anywhere else for that matter), make it a practice to pray over your food before you eat during mealtimes. People are watching you and how you live your life.

6. Lastly, start a prayer journal if you have not already done so, and keep track of how God answers your prayers about evangelism. You just may be surprised!

CHAPTER 5

ENGAGE...THROUGH RELATIONAL EVANGELISM

After sowing the last kernel of corn in my last field, I couldn't help but let out a huge sigh of relief. It had been a tough planting season. As I began the long drive back to the house, I felt the first few drops of water as a slow gentle rain began—there would be enough moisture for the seeds planted to germinate and grow. I couldn't have asked for a more timely blessing. I had prepared the soil to the best of my abilities, but now, I had to wait upon the process of nature before I could even think about reaping a harvest. That meant waiting for another six months before those same seeds I had just planted would turn into corn that I could harvest and take to market. Little did I know then that the Lord was preparing me for a lifetime of sowing seeds of a slightly different nature.

> ...relational evangelism has some realities that we should consider if we plan on making the most of our divine opportunities.

Five Realities of Relational Evangelism

Even though my farming experience happened years ago, the principles, or realities, for growing crops are still the same—prepare, plant, cultivate, harvest, and invest for the next crop. Relational evangelism requires some similarly great principles and I want to talk about five of these, which should help you as you practice your own personal evangelism. These five realities or principles are: prepare, plant, cultivate, harvest, and invest. Sound familiar? I should hope so! We'll take a look at how these five principles of relational evangelism can help us and how we already use them to some extent. But what is relational evangelism, and how can you do it? In the next few pages, I want you to join me as I share some personal insights and experiences in relational evangelism. This might help you see that it's okay to make mistakes—I still make a lot of them—and help you realize that the journey of relational evangelism can be just as fun and rewarding as harvest time itself. So, put on your best walking shoes and let's take a stroll through your harvest field—whether a rural community of close-knit families, the concrete jungle of an inner-city neighborhood, or the sprawling neighborhoods of suburban America.

Prepare – You need to build relationships

Many of us already enjoy building and nurturing relationships around our areas of work, play, and day-to-day activities. Whether the relationships are close or merely with a person we recognize and say hello to at the grocery store, we all have relationships. If you had to pick a person to share the Gospel with, it would probably be a person with whom you have built some level of relationship. Over the years, I have asked my evangelism students how many of them prefer the door-to-door, in your face, confrontational evangelism?

In all the years of teaching I have only had two students who raised their hands! Everyone else said they would rather share the Gospel in a more relational, one-on-one setting with someone they knew.

You might wonder how you build relationships for relational evangelism. My answer? The same way you developed the friends that you enjoy right now. Through the years you have met people in school and in other settings that grew into wonderful relationships. Great relationships take time, commitment, and intentionality—just like relational evangelism! Relational evangelism demands the intentional pursuit of trusted relationships because you may only see these people once or twice a week—even if they are your neighbor. That means you must work with intentionality toward making each encounter effective in strengthening that relationship. Building these kinds of relationships demands a bit of determination.

However, even if someone fails to cross the line of faith and ask Jesus Christ to be the Leader and Lord of his or her life in these relationships, that person should still be our friend. We should not build trusted relationships so that people can be used for our gain—how would you feel if someone did that to you? We must realize: *Building trusted friendships provides opportunities to speak into other people's lives and allows others to see God at work in you.* As Steve Sjogren said: "The trick of delivering God's mail to a person's spiritual address is really no trick at all; it's mostly a matter of caring enough to treat people with the kindness and respect we desire for ourselves."[86] Make sure you let God, not selfish motives, lead you in your pursuit of building trusted relationships, and be patient. Time can play a huge role in the influence we can have in our friendships. Just like an old friend of mine who I had been working on for over thirty years. Let me share the story with you.

---

86 Steve Sjogren, Dave Ping, & Doug Pollock, *Irresistible Evangelism: Natural Ways to Open Others to Jesus* (Loveland, CO: Group Publishing, 2004), 70.

I was in Orlando, Florida helping with a conference when I received a message on my cell phone that one of my old friends, Tim,[87] had called. I had been too busy earlier in the day to talk with him and planned to call him when I got back to the hotel. Tim is one of those slow works-in-progress that I believe God has been working on and is going to be a great testimony for God. Tim and I have been friends since high school, where I tutored him in algebra so he could pass the test and keep playing football. I was one of the few people that could talk to Tim and calm him down when he got mad—and it was never good when Tim got mad.

Over the years Tim would call occasionally, sometimes waiting for more than a year to call—I even visited him once in Arizona. We were friends, if only distant ones, but Tim always knew he could call me when he was in trouble, or when things got bad—like the time his brother committed suicide, and when he got divorced. Tim knew he could be himself when talking to me and that I didn't mind if he used a little profanity. Rick Richardson said it best when he stated: "The model of conversations with spiritual friends delights in the relationship itself and rejoices over every spiritual conversation."[88] I loved every opportunity to share with Tim what God had done in my life and left the pressure of whether Tim made a decision to follow Christ up to God. That's the beauty of relational evangelism—you just work on building new and stronger relationships and God brings natural, faith-sharing opportunities your way!

I finally called Tim back and found that he was doing fine, and we had some small talk about the conference I was attending. Tim knows that I am a minister now, and I always look forward

---

87   All names have been changed.

88   Rick Richardson, *Reimagining Evangelism: Inviting Friends On A Spiritual Journey* (Downers Grove: InterVarsity, 2006), 27.

to strengthening our friendship in hopes that God will give me opportunities to witness to him. This time was no exception. Tim had developed a close relationship with Rick Husband, the former NASA Shuttle commander, who was killed along with his crew when the Space Shuttle Columbia tragically burned up on re-entry. Rick's faith had been a powerful testimony to Tim, so talking about this accident always seemed to bring up questions about the Bible. That night was a bit different because Tim asked me whether I "really talked in tongues or not." I was able to talk with Tim about how close of a relationship the Lord desires for us to have with him and that speaking in tongues was often a believer praying in ways he or she did not understand as the Holy Spirit prompted him or her. I shared that many people abused this gift from the Lord, but it was a teaching embraced by the Pentecostal and charismatic churches. This gift was intended to exalt the Lord, not people, and help us grow in greater intimacy with God.

Then, Tim said he would like to sit down with me sometime to inquire about the Bible, as well as how and what he ought to read. I shared some Scriptures like Psalms 91 and 1 John 1:9 with him, as well as a few others, and told him to call me anytime, because I always had time to talk with him (contrary to what I wrote earlier about being too busy). I used some simple terminology like, letting God forgive us, and allowing Jesus to become the Leader of our lives—because a life led by God is always a lot better than when we try to lead ourselves. I told Tim that God cared about him and all that he did, and that God was always listening whenever Tim wanted to talk with Him. I told Tim we could talk to God just like we talk to one another and that God always wanted the best for us. We shared a little more small talk before hanging up.

A few years later I had the thrill of my life while eating dinner one night. The phone rang, and as usual, everyone thought it was a telemarketer. But to my surprise, Tim spoke up on the other end of the line. I shouted hello and asked him how he was doing. Tim said, "I just wanted to let you know that 'I'm in!'" I said, "What?" And again, Tim said, "I'm in," and proceeded to tell me how he had crossed the line of faith. I can't tell you how awesome that felt—to know after all these years that I would see my friend Tim in heaven. I had merely been one link in a long chain of people who had talked to Tim about Christ—all because I practiced relational evangelism. I just wanted to build a trusted friendship that would give me opportunities to speak into Tim's life whenever God orchestrated those divine appointments. I was Tim's friend because I wanted to be friends, not for what I could get from him—just another salvation decision. God used our friendship to prepare Tim, and me, for harvest time.

Plant – Anybody Can Do Nothing

A second reality or principle emerges with Scripture's exhortation in Matthew 28:19, "Therefore go and make disciples of all nations, baptizing them in the name of the Father and of the Son and of the Holy Spirit." This verse reveals the need for action because it tells us to "go," to "make," and to "baptize;" highlighting the importance of our actions. As disciplers, we will find, "what we are communicates far more eloquently than anything we say or do,"[89] revealing the value of emulating a Christ-filled life as we model and practice relational evangelism. Putting our words into action will speak loudly for those who practice relational evangelism, because for many people, "nonverbals tend to convey true meaning."[90] We

---

89   Stephen R. Covey, *The Seven Habits of Highly Effective People* (New York: Simon & Schuster, 1989), 22.

90   Julia A. Gorman, *Community That Is Christian*, 2nd ed (Grand Rapids, MI: Baker Books, 2002), 151.

must realize that other people are watching and listening to us in our lifestyles and not just in how we talk to other people. You may plant seeds in a person's life without even talking to them! If the truth be known, most of us eavesdrop on other people's conversations when they get loud enough. The same is true when God orchestrates a divine encounter for us to share the Gospel with someone.

We also need to quit criticizing our evangelism efforts. If you are honest with yourself, you don't always do evangelism right. And sadly, we may even do evangelism extremely wrong. Take my flight aboard a Chicago-bound plane wherein I sat next to a very nice young lady. As you read this story, try to think of what failures I experienced (that should be easy) and what successes I should feel good about after my flying evangelism experience.

As I boarded the small airplane on my way back home, I had the luck of being in seat "1B." After situating myself and stowing my laptop bag in an overhead compartment, I sat down with my laptop and book in hand with the hopes of doing a little work while in flight. I wondered whether I would have a seatmate or have the whole section to myself, but I did not have to wait long until a nice young lady indicated that she would be occupying the seat next to me. Thoughts of how I could initiate a conversation about spiritual matters began filling my mind. After all, I had just finished reading a great book on apologetics and evangelism. I thought I might enjoy the opportunity of seeing whether any of the insights I read would help me in this scenario. Sadly, the young lady quickly began perusing her secular magazines, and even when I asked interesting questions, or so I thought, the conversation floundered. Although the young lady was polite, she obviously cared less about my attempts at conversation.

Her receptivity was typical of many young business professionals. She did not know me and merely wanted to get home. At one point, after learning she lived in Chicago, I shared that I had recently been at Wheaton, hoping it would propel the spiritual conversation onward. But my hopes remained just that, so I inquired a bit about where in Chicago she lived and how she liked the city. By this time, I was just trying to be polite and not force a spiritual conversation. After our small talk the stewardess brought beverages around, and I settled in for some quality work time. I planned on typing up notes for a paper and in the midst of getting everything situated I spilled some ice out of my cup. So, I not only witnessed a conversation fizzle, but I had now spilled some ice on my newfound, not-so-friendly friend's feet. Luckily, she wore tennis shoes, and it appeared that the ice hit the floor of the airplane. As we started our final approach into the next airport my new acquaintance discovered, much to my horror, that one piece of ice had found its way into her open purse.

If I have ever experienced the old cliché "insult added to injury," this was it. I felt about three inches tall and apologized profusely, offering to get the stewardess's personal supply of napkins if needed. The young lady brushed off the enormity of the situation and simply said that it was not a "big deal," which obviously did not make me feel any better. I felt absolutely miserable with the results of my honest efforts at displaying proper airplane etiquette, and to a much lesser degree now, any evangelism opportunities that I had totally botched.

The reason I share this incident stems from our tendency as Christians to see evangelism as either success or failure. Success when Gospel presentations culminate in prayers of salvation, and failure with anything less. With this encounter, I had to pray hard to see the good that God could have used in that situation. But God uses our actions just as easily as He uses our words of Scripture, reasoning, or concern. A common cliché states that our "actions speak louder than words" and I wholeheartedly agree—especially because non-Christians often have preconceived ideas or stereotypes about how Christians think, act, and feel.

After my disastrous airplane flight, I began to realize that God could easily use numerous pieces of our conversation. Since I had mentioned my attendance at Wheaton, she might realize I was a Christian. Anyone living in the Chicago area would know about Wheaton College and its reputation within the community, and this young lady quickly responded that she knew where the college was located early in our conversation. But perhaps I merely needed to model Christianity at this stage in her spiritual journey. Perhaps I revealed that not all Christians have abrasive personalities or try to force spiritual conversations on people, and that Christians can even be sensitive, caring, and apologetic. God may actually be big enough to use the things I do not say to speak very loudly to those who lack familiarity with today's Church.

In the end, God has called each of us to scatter seeds of faith, hope, and God's love. God will do whatever else is needed if we will allow God an opportunity to use us. Understanding the Gospel obviously helps Christians share their faith when opportunities present themselves, but oftentimes knowing when not to share anything except the actions of God's love may be even more powerful. Christians believe, and especially Pentecostal Christians, that they have been endued with supernatural power from God to share the Gospel. This same Gospel must be shared and demonstrated in our words and everyday actions, and should not be seen as difficult.

In John 1:7, John the Baptist came "to testify concerning the light." In the original Greek language, the word *testify* implies having something good to say about someone. Christians do this by giving a "witness" or "testimony" of what God has done in their lives. Saying something good about God and what he has done in your life can be effective—and what Christian has nothing good to say about what Christ has done in his or her life? Every Christian can easily "do" evangelism if they would willingly share something good that God has done in their lives whenever God opens a window of opportunity—it is just that simple. Similarly, living out

Christian values in our everyday lives speaks loudly to those around us, conveying a witness of what God has done in our lives. The Gospel changes our desires, our actions, and us.

Cultivate Relationships When Opportunities Arise

Cultivating relationships is the third principle or reality in relational evangelism. This can pose special challenges today since a lot of younger people describe Christianity as "hypocritical, judgmental, too political and out of touch with reality."[91] Trying to build trusted relationships with cynical people who have been hurt by the Church will demand the love of Jesus Christ and lots of patience. Over time your non-judgmental attitude and desire to listen and help—as a friend—will eventually remove the barriers to more meaningful conversations. Sometimes, your actions will impact other people who are unchurched, but your actions may also affect people who already serve in their local churches.

Relational evangelism does not have to specifically target only unchurched people. So many people in the church long for a compassionate, loving touch from God, and sometimes, much to my amazement, God uses common, everyday Christians to do just that. God has called us to scatter the seed, and when Gospel seed is scattered, some will land on rocky, thorny, and other less-than-favorable places. Even when seeds are scattered in good soil, healthy plants still need nurturing, by cultivating and removing weeds that grow up and try to choke the growing plants. This is a principle I discovered long ago.

---

91   David Kinnaman with Aly Hawkins, *You Lost Me: Why Young Christians Are Leaving Church…and Rethinking Faith* (Grand Rapids, MI: BakerBooks, 2011), 20.

When I was about thirteen, my dad gave me fifteen acres of corn to care for as my own. I was thrilled with such an opportunity to make some money and have something that was mine. The ground was prepared and planted for me, so all I had to do was cultivate it when the corn began to grow. To help you grasp the size of that undertaking you should realize that engineers use an average city block calculation of one hundred thousand square feet, which is about two and a half acres—or six city blocks in most cities for my fifteen acres. For football fans, you know that a football field is 300 feet long by 160 feet wide, which is about 1.1 acres. I began the arduous task of hoeing the entire cornfield—not quite 14 football fields—after school and on the weekends, but I never dreamed that hoeing could take so much time! That cornfield looked enormous, and I thought I would never finish hoeing that field. When I finished cultivating about two-thirds of the field, my dad helped me learn a valuable lesson. He let me stop hoeing!

Initially, I thought I had just received the greatest gift I could have gotten that summer. However, I discovered that the weeds soon grew thick where my hoeing and cultivating had ceased. By the end of the growing season my precious, uncultivated corn was stunted and far less fruitful than my cultivated plants. Seeing those stunted corn plants solidified the reality that even the best of crops—and Christians—need a little hoeing every now and then.

Harvest Time Takes Time

Waiting is the fourth and hardest reality of evangelism, but you must remember that God did not ask you to "win" souls. He just asked you to plant seeds. Steve Sjogren and evangelism author George G. Hunter III estimate that, "on average, it takes between twelve and twenty significant 'Gospel touches' for people to move from the beginning of the scale into genuine relationships with Christ."[92] So don't beat yourself up! Didn't Paul say, "Let us not be weary in doing good, for at the proper time we will reap a harvest if we do not give up" (Galatians 6:9)? The Apostle Paul was encouraging the Galatians when they faced people who were bogged down in sin and needed correction, but this truth applies to every aspect of our lives—including relational evangelism. Relational evangelism involves building trusted relationships, because you have to earn the right to speak into someone's life on a deep spiritual level. This is the level of core beliefs for most people and allowing anyone close proximity can be a very scary thing. So, building life-long friendships actually opens the door to evangelism with many of our friends that we have known for years—like my friend Bob, who had lived a difficult life.

Bob recently called unexpectedly and left a message for me. He indicated his need to talk and asked me to give him a call when I got a chance. His voice sounded serious, so I prayed a bit prior to calling since I was unsure of what to expect. I knew that Bob had lived like his money would never end, but unexpectedly, that is exactly what had happened. When his mother died, she left all of her inheritance to others—not her son. That alone would shock anyone, but apparently this only began a journey that would lead our paths to cross.

When I called Bob, we exchanged the usual pleasantries and tried to catch up on all that had transpired since high school. Surprisingly, Bob shared that although he had been divorced twice and lived quite the profligate lifestyle, he still felt as though he had never lost his faith. We chatted briefly on what that meant, and during the course of our conversation, Bob shared that he felt something was just "missing." He did not really know how to express in words what

---

92   Sjogren, Ping, & Pollock, 53.

he was feeling so we talked for a while about his "faith" and how he viewed religion. During this conversation, Bob shared that he had never really focused on the Jesus of the New Testament, because he felt that if God was the "boss" then you should just go to Him.

When Bob stated, "I have never really given Jesus Christ a lot of thought," I realized that Jesus was exactly what he had been missing throughout his entire life. I proceeded to share the Scriptures that I felt might help Bob in his understanding of Christ and what role He plays in a personal relationship with God. But even as I shared the Gospel, I sensed a struggle on the other end of the phone line. This seemed like something new to Bob and I could tell he needed time to explore and see how Jesus fit into his world. I did not force Bob to say a prayer of dedication or confess his sins right there on the phone, but I did ask him if it was alright if I prayed with him about allowing Jesus Christ to truly take on the role of leader and lord of his life.

We prayed together and afterwards I thanked Bob for the privilege of praying with him. He said that he really appreciated it and that "actually, that's one of the best prayers I've ever had." This only confirmed that Bob had the knowledge of God and his Son, Jesus Christ, but he lacked the heart knowledge, or faith, necessary to let Jesus Christ have Lordship of his life. I encouraged Bob's attendance at a local church I knew in his area, and I gave him some readings in the New Testament to work through as he explored the Scriptures concerning Jesus Christ. I told him to call me if he had any questions and we said our goodbyes.

Some Convictions on Conversion

As I look back on that experience with Bob, I realize other Christians might see this exchange as a Gospel success. The Gospel was presented, and the prayer of salvation was prayed (for the most part). But I tend to see these kinds of divine appointments differently.

Bob just happened to be in a place on his spiritual journey where he needed answers and sought them in people that he trusted. I did not sense that an actual conversion took place, but that I was able to provide honest, thought-provoking insights into what might be the spiritually missing link in Bob's life. I provided truths that God could use long after Bob and I ended our discussion.

I must confess my conviction that God the Father, God the Son, and God the Holy Spirit arises as the only "soul-winner" from Scripture. John 3:16 states: "For God so loved the world that he gave his one and only Son, that whoever believes in him shall not perish but have eternal life." Jesus said in John 3:5, "I tell you the truth, no one can enter the kingdom of God unless he is born of water and the Spirit." Titus 3:5b states, "He saved us through the washing of rebirth and renewal by the Holy Spirit," and the Apostle Paul shares in Romans 8:11, "And if the Spirit of him who raised Jesus from the dead is living in you, he who raised Christ from the dead will also give life to your mortal bodies through his Spirit, who lives in you" (NIV). All this reveals that humankind cannot in and of itself regenerate anyone. God has reserved that work for Himself and His Holy Spirit. Thus, we can declare with the Apostle Paul in 2 Corinthians 5:17, "Therefore, if anyone is in Christ, he is a new creation; the old has gone, the new has come!" Paul even stated in 1 Corinthians 3:6, "I planted the seed, Apollos watered it, but God made it grow." Truly, God remains the only "soul-winner" in the process of conversion.

I appreciate the comparison made by Steve Sjogren between marriage and conversion, and that "When we rightly understand evangelism, we recognize that it is both a miracle and a mystery how any of us come to know Christ."[93] How true that something

---

93 Steve Sjogren, *Conspiracy of Kindness: a refreshing new approach to sharing the love of Jesus*, revised ed (Ventura, CA: Regal, 2003), 134.

as serious and life-changing as inviting Jesus Christ into your life should not be considered so trivial that a fifteen or twenty minute presentation allows an appropriate amount of time to make such a significant decision. God can obviously work miracles even in fifteen or twenty minutes, but Christianity is not some beverage ordered at a fast food restaurant's drive up window. It is unquestionably the most important decision a person can make, and one that should be made with significant information and consideration. Christians must prepare themselves to share the Gospel in hopes that they may be the final link in the series of spiritual encounters a person faces when moving toward understanding the Gospel message and making a salvation decision.

So, while I had the privilege of sharing the Gospel with my friends from high school, God alone reserves conversion and regeneration to Himself. After all, having someone call you and ask about Christianity is exponentially easier for most people than initiating conversations in confrontational evangelism. But in all honesty, we have given confrontational evangelism a bad reputation—usually due to some people with very abrasive personalities. Confrontational evangelism merely reflects a method of evangelism in which someone actively approaches an individual they usually do not know in order to share the Gospel message with them. They are initiators of Gospel conversations that usually emerge as questions, which will hopefully lead those individuals toward an understanding that God loves them and longs for them to have a personal relationship with Him through His son Jesus Christ. These people are extroverts who love the excitement and challenge that confrontational evangelism can bring. They passionately believe in a literal hell that every non-Christian will face unless they make a decision for Christ and cannot wait to tell others about what Christ has done in their lives.

However, with relational evangelism, patience is a reality you must embrace. My friendship with Tim opened the door to a thirty-year relationship, earning me the right to speak into his life. My friendship with Bob opened a door to faithfully sow some Gospel seeds, while pondering whether I had shared the right things and chastising myself later for the things I had forgotten. Yes, I still chastise myself at missed opportunities, but God reminds me that He is in control and He will water the seeds sown in His time. Like links in a chain, every person sharing or acting out the Gospel stands as an equal partner. All the links are important and every one of them plays a strategic role, which leads to a uniquely different perspective on my return flight home earlier in this chapter that had spilled ice and failure written all over it.

Invest in Yourself

One more principle or reality awaits us if we truly desire effectiveness in our efforts at relational evangelism. Since relational evangelism flows out of your relationship with Christ, it makes sense for us to invest in our own spiritual wellbeing. Our Christlikeness will attract other people! Jesus said, "And I, when I am lifted up [exalted] from the earth, will draw all people to myself" (John 12:32). Christ does this through the gift of God's Holy Spirit. Jesus also said in John 6:44, "No one can come to me unless the Father who has sent me draws them, and I will raise them up at the last day." The Scriptures reveal that when we lift up Christ, the Holy Spirit will do the drawing! How crucial for you and me to be witnesses in our words, our actions, and our attitude. This fifth and final reality of relational evangelism is as important as all the other realities I have talked about and should involve some serious spiritual planning.

Some common sense in the area of relational evangelism will include caring not only for your spiritual development, but also your physical wellbeing. If you don't normally take care of yourself on the outside—or physically—why should someone look at you and want to hear what you have to say about your spiritual convictions? Failing to invest in yourself physically may actually put up a wall of resistance to any kind of evangelism, no matter what level of spiritual maturity you feel you have achieved. This may seem petty, but if people find you unpleasant to be around, it will be exponentially more difficult to influence them in their spiritual beliefs.

Obviously, investing in your spiritual wellbeing remains paramount, and we must strategically approach this aspect of our spiritual formation through spiritual disciplines. Dallas Willard, discussing the contrast between human spiritual formation and Christian spiritual formation, said: "Christian spiritual formation, in contrast, is the *redemptive process of forming the inner human world so that it takes on the character of the inner being of Christ himself.*"[94] So you must focus on Christian spiritual development— not just human spiritual development. Willard then emphasizes fasting and Scripture memorization in the process of Christian spiritual formation. These two facets of spiritual development are often overlooked—and in many cases ignored, helping us see that spiritual disciplines often require hard work, or discipline, to weave them into our daily lives. These disciplines will equip you for greater impact as you model a Christian lifestyle to friends and family.

Since spiritual warfare challenges evangelism on several fronts, fasting, Scripture memorization, and prayer become powerful disciplines. There are many wonderful resources and books available on fasting, which bring awareness to the different types of fasts and how to fast responsibly when diet restrictions and health issues are involved. Scripture memorization is something you can do each week and helps us say with the Psalmist, "I have hidden your word in my heart that I might not sin against you" (Psalm 119:11).

---

94   Dallas Willard, *The Great Omission* (San Francisco: Harper, 2006), 105.

And prayer lies at the heart of our spiritual relationship with God, awakening us to the reality that, "The most important thing in spiritual warfare is the power found in the name of Jesus Christ."[95]

The disciplines of mandatory reflection and prayer are two of the greatest benefits to spiritual planning. You should regularly spend time in prayerful reflection to help you gain the awareness of what is lacking in your spiritual life. Spiritual disciplines do not revolve solely around Scripture, prayer, and church attendance, but spiritual disciplines involve every aspect of your life. Being a Godly witness should include regular times of prayer and spiritual assessment, because we are called to be witnesses to the world, not ourselves. Spiritual disciplines can involve quality family times, fun times, Christian friends, personal acquaintances, and even your secular job. You may even enjoy some of the numerous tools available today that help you gain a proper evaluation of your spiritual condition. But, the most valuable tool of all remains the Holy Spirit who will guide you unto all truths as you seek Him in prayer.

---

95 Wonsuk Ma, William W. Menzies, and Hyeon-sung Bae, *David Yonggi Cho: A Close Look at His Theology & Ministry* (Baguio City, Philippines: APTS Press, 2004), 53.

SUMMARY

Today's church leaders and disciplers often elaborate on the many excuses and fears that prevail in evangelism, but every Christian needs to remember, "winning the world to Jesus Christ begins with one soul at a time."[96] As I reflected upon the situations with my friend Bob or the young lady on my flight, my early discipleship training falsely presented these as dichotomous examples of success and failure. With Bob, I may have been the last link in the chain on his spiritual journey; with the young lady, I may have just needed to model Christianity. With Tim, we can see that relational evangelism is about building relationships and planting seeds—you cannot judge yourself in evangelism as a success or failure. The Devil has used that mentality to discourage multitudes of great evangelists—just like you! So, pick up your bag of Gospel seed and start sowing seed wherever you go. There are people in your community who have been waiting to hear some Good News from someone they trust.

---

96   Scott G. Wilkins, *Reach: A Team Approach to Evangelism and Assimilation* (Grand Rapids, MI: Baker Books, 2005), 134.

YOUR ASSIGNMENT:
Reflection, Sharing, And Application
(with a group or alone)

1. Write down or share in a group at least one person you already know on a first name basis at a place you frequent every week for whom you could begin praying. This can include anyone from airport staff to the staff at your favorite restaurant—or even the local hardware store or coffee shop workers. Where to you go each week?

2. Think about or discuss with your group these places you routinely visit and how you might build relationships with people there. Bank tellers, grocery store cashiers, Post Office employees, students or teachers at schools, retail store employees, and peers at work are some of the type of people with whom great relationships can be nurtured!

3. Write down or share in a group unpleasant evangelism situations you may have had that you thought were total failures. What positive aspects of those experiences can you or your group see that may help reveal what God might have done in spite of your efforts?

4. Mark Mittelberg[97] mentions having three people for whom you readily pray concerning faith in Christ. Make your own list right now of three people you know.

    a. _____

    b. _____

    c. _____

---

97   Bill Hybels and Mark Mittelberg, *Becoming A Contagious Christian* (Grand Rapids, MI: Zondervan, 1994), 104.

5. Share how you would translate the following verse in the King James translation of Scripture into more modern language so that non-churched people might understand.

    a. John 3:16, "For God so loved the world, that He gave His only begotten Son, that whosoever believeth in Him should not perish, but have everlasting life."

CHAPTER 6

ASK

L.E.**A**.R.N. Evangelism means to:

ASK – Asking questions is an easy way to start conversations.

Questions are a wonderful way to start conversations without offense, uncover faulty thinking, encourage better alternatives, and allow people to come to a better decision by themselves. Most people would rather come to a conclusion themselves as opposed to someone else telling them what is right and wrong—and questions are a great way to do that. There are many different authors who have written some wonderful insights on the use of questions with various names: questioning evangelism and conversational evangelism just to name a couple.

Greg Koukl does an exceptional job of highlighting some simple steps of rational discussion in his book, *Tactics: A Game Plan for Discussing Your Spiritual Convictions,* that will help expose the inconsistencies of other religions and ideologies. His simple approach of humbly asking key questions, educating ourselves in our own beliefs, and doing a little detective work often helps us lead others to the truths of Scripture. Koukl's book presents itself as a non-threatening approach to apologetics that most "followers of Jesus Christ" can easily embrace. He states: "In this book I would like to teach you how to be diplomatic. I want to suggest a method I call the Ambassador Model. This approach trades more on friendly curiosity—a kind of relaxed diplomacy—than on confrontation."[98] Taking the pressure out of one-on-one evangelism is the beginning of evangelism happiness!

Norman and David Geisler share similar insights in their book, *Conversational Evangelism*, which involves the use of questions. They state: "In brief, Conversational Evangelism involves listening carefully to others and *hearing* the discrepancies in their views and then *illuminating* those discrepancies by asking questions to help clarify their religious terminology and *expose* the weaknesses of their perspective. Then, we want to dig up their history and uncover their underlying barriers to *build* a bridge to the Gospel (1 Corinthians 3:6)."[99] Using this approach puts the pressure on us to educate ourselves in order to ask those thought-provoking questions, which will open the door to further questions and bridge-building opportunities to the Gospel of Jesus Christ.

Thankfully, you can also merely allow questions to arise naturally. When you engage people about their faith, you should eventually ask simple questions to help steer the conversation toward spiritual matters. If you are a good listener and the person you are with brings up some struggles in his or her life, you may just ask a question: "Have you ever prayed about stuff like that?" "Is your church family helping you during this tough time?" If the answer is negative, you can share about how God has answered prayers for you or how your church family has been such a tremendous blessing to you. Here are some other possible questions:

---

98 Gregory Koukl, *Tactics: A Game Plan For Discussing Your Christian Convictions* (Grand Rapids: Zondervan, 2009), 20.

99 Norman Geisler and David Geisler, *Conversational Evangelism* (Eugene, OR: Harvest House, 2009), 118.

- Have you ever thought about how God could bless your life?
- Is there anything special I can pray with you about?
- Have you ever, honestly, made peace with God?
- Where do you go to church?
- Do you ever struggle with finding peace in a world of constant change?
- Are you really happy with your life right now?
- Have you ever thought about faith issues?
- What do you think the word *salvation* means?
- Have you ever thought about eternity?
- If something terrible were to happen, do you have a peace about where you would spend eternity?
- Has anyone ever really taken the time to share with you what Christianity is all about?
- Have you ever thought much about matters of faith and spirituality?
- Has anyone ever shared with you who Jesus Christ really is?
- Have you found any good Bibles or devotions for your phone or computer?
- Do you ever pray about things that are going on at school / work?
- Do you ever wonder if there's a God who really cares about us?
- What do you think about (the latest news story about faith issues or the church that may be in the newspaper or on television)? This could be a great way to confront negative issues in the church and talk about how different your church family—and true Christianity—is pertaining to that issue.

Your listening skills and the Holy Spirit will guide you in asking the right questions. Honestly, your creativity is the only limitation to the questions you can ask!

No matter how you feel best suited to share the Gospel, be sincere and sensitive to the convictions of others. If you truly care, that will be obvious through your actions, voice, and conversation. I love how the Message Bible translates Proverbs 25:11-13.

The right word at the right time is like a custom-made piece of jewelry, And a wise friend's timely reprimand is like a gold ring slipped on your finger. Reliable friends who do what they say are like cool drinks in sweltering heat—refreshing!

When we ask the Holy Spirit to guide our conversations and questions about faith issues, we'll be seen as a refreshing, cool drink in the really difficult times of life. A timely word is a word spoken or read at just the right time in a person's life. When that happens, we'll usually find appreciation from others because we took that step of faith to reach out and share a caring word of comfort to someone in need.

Think of your favorite hobbies, sports, or job-related activities to which you could draw spiritual parallels. Try to read about current events when you can so that you are familiar with your community's issues. Then, in the course of talking shop or another one of your more enjoyable activities, ask a question that connects an activity or situation to a spiritual truth. Then see what God does! Most importantly, you need to be yourself—don't try to be something or someone you are not. Additionally, don't beat yourself up if you feel like you may have not shared superbly! As a matter of fact, this seems to happen to me quite often.

When I first returned home from serving in the Armed Forces, I decided I needed to plug into a church since I had recently come back into a right relationship with the Lord. The church I attended had a discipleship program that I participated in for two years—growing in my faith and Scripture memorization. Little did I realize that this discipleship class was a great foundation for the next phase of my life. There was an Evangelism Explosion (EE) group at this church and someone must have eventually talked me into joining, because I don't think I would have done that to myself! When I first started attending the EE classes, the presentation of the Gospel seemed very structured and almost cold. But I realized, as time when on, that learning a specific presentation was merely a means of helping me see the goal and one method of presenting the Gospel story. Over time I realized that how I arrived at the goal was inconsequential as long as I was able to sow some spiritual seeds.

So, what am I saying? I'm saying that you are different from every other person on this planet—and that's a wonderful thing! Because we are all different, we share important news differently and relate easier with people more like us. Brick layers can relate to brick layers, actors can relate to actors, financial investors can relate to other financial investors, lawyers are often respected by, and can relate to, other lawyers, and so on. That's not a bad thing to be different, but it is a reality that we should remind ourselves of on occasion. That's why I mentioned above not to beat yourself up for what you haven't done. Be yourself and ask the Holy Spirit for an extra special nudge if you are prone to a high level of "ignore-ance," which my wife, Nancy, has informed me of at times.

We should work to let Gospel conversations arise naturally in our regular conversations and interactions with others. Just dropping little comments like: "I think I better pray about that;" or "Pray for me will you? I've got to see the boss today;" or "Wow! I've been praying for new clients all week and today God has really answered my prayers!" "By the way, how can I pray for you? What do you think about prayer?" By sharing these short comments or asking questions, you can bring up sensitive issues of faith, as well as help that person realize that you genuinely care about them and where they are in their spiritual journey. Then just be a friend and don't unload on them—share as the Holy Spirit leads you, which is usually in short snippets.

Witnessing Encounters

An interesting witnessing encounter occurred while I was flying to Orlando, Florida. When boarding the plane, I found myself sitting next to a young man and woman. This was a somewhat larger plane than normal for the small airport I was flying out of, so I was pleasantly surprised at the increased room. I had just been praying that the Lord would direct my path so that I could witness to someone and I wondered what the Lord had in store for me. Taking the initiative, and being a very social person, I introduced myself and found that I was sitting next to Jim and Beth. I began to continue the conversation in hopes that the Lord might allow it to turn towards spiritual matters. Jim and Beth were eager to visit, and I discovered that he was a high school Senior, who loved the drums and would be attending a local university the next year. He and his sister Beth, who was a Junior in high school and played trumpet just like I did, were from a town near my home. When they told me that, I knew this was a divine appointment. Our family just so happened to have services at the church in that community the very next Sunday and I just knew that God would work it out so that they could join us—but I was wrong.

After we got through the surprise of all that we had in common, I asked where they were going. Jim said that they were going to meet their dad, who they had never met before. They were raised by their mom and step-dad, who they said was a great father to them. Needless to say, they were a bit nervous. They appeared to be nice young people, but I could tell God and church were not their number one interest in life—they were not even sure where the church I would speak at was located in their town, even though it is located on the main street going into town (and the town is not that big). I was able to share about the peace and comfort that God could bring in those kinds of situations; and encouraged them to hold on to God throughout their visit. The both said that they were going to come to the services the following Sunday to see us, and I encouraged them to do so. I gave them one of our prayer cards and told Jim to keep in touch so that I could find out how things went—he said he would.

Several things struck me during the week that followed. First, I really kicked myself for not taking the risk to bluntly ask whether they had a relationship with God or not, and if not, was there any reason they wouldn't want to have that. But I always seem to err on the side of trying not to offend people and I was hoping our conversation would continue in the days to come. I also did not feel the Holy Spirit prompting me to push them into a corner. Second, my young friends never came to the services, which confirmed even more that I should always "take the risk" when in the middle of a faith conversation instead of waiting for an opportunity that may never come. Finally, I never received a phone call or email. So, I must be content with knowing that I at least sowed some Gospel seeds. Honestly, that is all God has asked us to do. We cannot change anyone's heart—that change can only happen when someone willingly asks forgiveness of sins and invites Jesus Christ to have Lordship and leadership of their lives.

The Lord gave me a neat revelation about my encounter with Jim and Beth. As we were exiting the plane, I became separated from them. When I actually walked out into the terminal, I noticed a gentleman in a nice western shirt, blue jeans, and cowboy boots standing there looking in my direction. He was obviously waiting for someone, and a bit out of the normal attire for that part of the country. I didn't think much about it.

I suddenly remembered I had not said goodbye to Jim and Beth, so I turned around to wait for them and encourage them one more time. When I turned around, I saw them in a group hug with the man who I had noticed earlier in the western attire. In that moment, the Holy Spirit reminded me that coming back to Christ was just like that picture of my seatmates and their biological dad who they had never seen. Seeing them there, reminded me of God's love for His children and how He wants to embrace all who come back to Him.

It also reminds me still today of how important it is to follow the commands of Christ and look for opportunities to help people come back into a right relationship with their heavenly Father. I love what Henry T. Blackaby shared in his book, *Created To Be God's Friend,* about obedience: "The first step toward being a 'friend of God' is obedience to 'follow Him' wherever He commands, wherever He goes, and wherever He should direct."[100] The closer we move toward Christ, the more we'll want what He wants, and the more we'll seek out His guidance no matter where it leads.

Sometimes we get confronted with the "rules" argument, or we may actually feel this way ourselves when talking about obedience to Christ. Some people get upset when trying to have faith conversations, because they see Christianity as just a bunch of rules that take all the fun out of life. However, I really appreciate what Greg Laurie states about that argument. You should not "emphasize what you gave up for God but rather what he gave up for you."[101]

When I think about this aspect of Christianity, I'm reminded of my wife, Nancy. We met when she was working on her Ph.D. in Curriculum and Instruction with an emphasis in Elementary Education at the University of Missouri in Columbia, Missouri. After teaching for almost fifteen years, she decided that she wanted to help other students realize their dream of becoming educators. Nancy was no stranger to hard work. Coming from a retired military family, she learned the value of hard work early in life. This helped her become one of the first in her family to

---

100 Henry T. Blackaby, *Created To Be God's Friend* (Nashville, TN: Thomas Nelson, 1999), 55.

101 Laurie, *How To Share Your Faith*, 42.

attend college at "Hard Work U," otherwise known as College of the Ozarks in Hollister, Missouri.

Nancy graduated and began her teaching career, while also attending night classes to earn her Master of Education degree. When we met, she was finishing up her dissertation project in her education doctoral program. We fell in love, got married in a very simple ceremony, and began following the Lord in ministry right after she received her degree. Shortly thereafter, Nancy began to feel the Lord dealing with her about putting her Ph.D. and career on the shelf while raising our two children. I realize not many folks have this luxury, but Nancy sensed the Lord speaking to her very clearly about this and I felt that I should trust the Lord as we stepped out in faith and worked various additional jobs to make ends meet.

The lesson for me was pretty clear: When you love someone enough and something is important enough, you are willing to sacrifice for what is best. That doesn't make it any easier to set something aside that you have worked your whole life for, and then put your efforts into something else that requires a huge step of faith. But when you know it is what God wants, you also realize it is something better than what you currently have, and a prayerful decision is needed. It has to be your choice, not something that is forced on you. As Nancy and I prayed about this decision, the Lord continued to give us a peace that passed human understanding and confirm that it was the right decision. Jim Collins aptly states: "Greatness is not a function of circumstance. Greatness, it turns out, is largely a matter of conscious choice."[102] Moving from good to great may be a secular term, but in God's perspective, when we move from our will to His, we have done exactly that. Nancy and I

---

102 Collins, Jim, *Good to Great: Why Some Companies Make the Leap...and Others Don't* (New York: HarperCollins, 2001), 11.

never desired greatness. We just wanted to follow God's leading for our lives. Looking back, we both agree that obedience was the key.

I realize that obedience to God's leading in reaching out to others is often a step of faith. But what a privilege we have to share our faith journey with someone who has taken a detour in life—or never even heard the Gospel message. I'm sure that in my story about Jim, Beth, and their biological father, both father—and children—were anxious about that first meeting, but repairing their relationship was more important to them than their anxieties. So too, many are anxious about that first meeting with a holy God. Talking with someone who has already met him—you, may just be what they need to cross that line of faith and place their trust in Jesus Christ. That's why obedience on our part is so important—eternity for someone is at stake.

I also think we fail to realize the power of asking God for opportunities to share our faith. So many Christians feel that since they are not really skilled at presenting the Gospel message to someone else, then they shouldn't even ask God for opportunities. Sadly, there are many people who are just waiting for someone like you to reach out in faith and share a word of hope. That word may be the word that opens a door of opportunity for some important faith conversations to take place and bring restoration to someone you know. Don't wait until you're an expert at witnessing—we have enough experts. What God really needs is someone who will sincerely pray for opportunities to share the love of Christ to a world that desperately needs Him, in his or her own way. You can do this—and God's got you covered!

On another flight, I happened to sit next to an older lady named Carol. I thought this was somewhat humorous because all the way out to my previous destination no one sat next to me—I had the whole section to myself, which was good because I was getting ready for a class. Carol was quite the crusty lady and not afraid to tell you so. She was a talker and even though the flight was not full, I felt like I was supposed to stay seated next to her. She had been married before and was from the northeast. She had been with her current boyfriend, Phil, for about 15 years. She did not really like where she lived and had been out East for about a month helping her family, which was a very close-knit group. Carol was the kind of lady that worked hard for what she acquired, and nobody was taking it from her. I listened a lot more than I talked, but we were able to visit about how sometimes it just seems like God was nowhere in sight and doesn't even care. I shared how I was surprised to find that God really did care about us and wanted to be involved in our lives—even with the little things in life.

We also talked about other issues she was dealing with: About how painful divorce is and how God won't make another person do something they don't want—that everyone has a free will and how the decisions of others can terribly hurt those that are closest to them. We also talked about how the fear of getting hurt again was what probably kept her from a blessed relationship. I was able to share with her how much the Lord really cared about her and how sometimes we just need to ask the Lord to take things away that aren't good for us. I encouraged her to ask the Lord to reveal anything that might be holding her back in her relationship—and what barriers might be keeping her from trusting God as much as she should.

She talked about the church back home and how disappointed she was there and had not been able to find a church she liked. She talked a bit about a local church I knew, and I told her she ought to go there and visit. I told her I dared her. She laughed and said she just might go. I gave Carol one of my cards and I asked her if I could pray with her and she said yes. We prayed and landed a short time later. I didn't get to see who she was meeting but really felt elated that God had allowed me an opportunity to help someone get a little closer to their heavenly Father just by asking some simple questions and listening.

Sharing Your Own Testimony

After you ask some questions that the Holy Spirit might put on your heart, you might want to share your own testimony. Like: "Yes, I remember when God first got a hold of me..." Make sure that you are in a place and have the time to share your testimony (see chapter ten for insights on writing yours). Trying to do this at work, while you are on the employer's time, is not a good time for lengthy sharing, plus it is not a good witness for you as a Christian either.

No matter whether you are asking questions or sharing your testimony, we need to talk in a language that the listener will understand. Are you talking to a doctor? Your language may articulate the finer points of archeological discoveries that have confirmed many of the Bible's teachings and use a higher level of the common language of your country. Are you talking to the homeless person who never finished high school? Your choice of words will either turn away or engage this person in a meaningful conversation that has the potential of changing their heart and opening their eyes to a brand-new way of life!

Myron Augsburger is a Mennonite pastor who shared a refreshing view of evangelism. He wrote, along with Clavin Ratz and Frank Tillapaugh in their book, *Mastering Outreach & Evangelism*, a chapter entitled: *Preaching Evangelistically*. He recounts the following encounter he had with a gentleman one day.

> Fond of theology as I am, I was tempted to describe to him the theological meaning of the atonement. Instead, I said, "Do you have some close friends?" When he nodded yes, I continued, "Suppose one of them gets in trouble. What are you going to do with him?"

> "Help him out," he said.

"How long are you going to hang in?"

"Well, he's your friend. You hang in."

"But he gets in worse trouble still. When can you cop out?"

A little peeved, he said, "Man, if he's your friend, you don't cop out. Even criminals won't cop out."

I looked at him and said, "And God came to us as a friend and identified with us in our problem. When can he cop out?"

"You mean Jesus?" he asked.

"Yes. If he's a friend, when can he say, 'That's it. I've gone far enough with you'?"

All at once, lights went on in his eyes, and he said, "You mean that's why Jesus had to die?"

"That's one reason. He couldn't cop out short of death, or else he wasn't really hanging in with you."

He stood up and dusted off his pants. Then he grinned at me and walked off down the street, squaring his shoulders as he went. As I watched him walk away, I muttered to him (although he couldn't hear), "You don't know it, but you've been evangelized."[103]

---

103 Calvin Ratz, Frank Tillapaugh, and Myron Augsburger, "Preaching Evangelistically" in *Mastering Outreach and Evangelism,* (Portland, OR: Multnomah, 1990), 144.

Talking in someone else's language goes a long way in helping them realize the relevance and reality of what a relationship with Jesus Christ can mean in their own lives. Our responsibility lies in sharing with a sincere heart and then letting God take over. Asking questions is just one of the many ways to humbly invite another person to talk about their beliefs in hopes that God will steer that conversation toward matters of faith. I hope you'll jump in head first.

YOUR ASSIGNMENT:
Reflection, Sharing, And Application

1. Write down four or five questions that would not only be relevant where you live and work, but also be possible transition questions that could lead to further conversations about a person's faith journey.

2. Make as least one effort this week to ask someone a question that could lead to further discussion about spiritual matters.

3. Tell someone you know what you are planning to do so that they can hold you accountable. This will also give you someone to tell what happened!

4. If you are in a group setting, share some experiences you had this past week to encourage others or enlist prayer for discouraging encounters you may have had. Regardless of how your encounter went, rejoice that you have made the effort to scatter some Gospel seed.

5. If you are in a group setting, role play on asking different questions in different scenarios. You just might have a few laughs while you are doing it!

6. One of the most important things you can do is write out your testimony. Most people "know" what God has done in their lives, but when they try to articulate that in a discussion it often does not happen as smoothly as originally thought. This may take several pages but that's o.k. If you need additional insights, take a peek at chapter ten.

7. Now that you have written out your testimony, write it again in one paragraph! This way, you can share your testimony whether you just have minutes—or hours.

CHAPTER 7

ASK...BECAUSE IT'S ALL ABOUT THE FISH

Growing up on the farm, I loved fishing. We would grab our poles and head to the small lake we had on the place. As a young boy, I always enjoyed the smells of the lake, the fish, and the forest, in addition to being alone with nature. But the really exhilarating feeling was when I felt a nibble on my lure and then the tug of a fish on the line! The thrill of catching a fish brought with it a feeling that is still hard for me to describe today. But one thing I know; it sure stirred up a passion to keep fishing!

> Matthew 4:19, "And he said to them, 'Follow me, and I will make you fishers of men.'"

It may come as no great surprise, that many people have likened sharing one's faith in Christ with others as a type of fishing—much like Jesus himself did. In Matthew 4:18-20, we're told: "While walking by the Sea of Galilee, he saw two brothers, Simon (who is called Peter) and Andrew his brother, casting a net into the sea, for they were fishermen. And he said to them, 'Follow me, and I will make you fishers of men.' Immediately they left their nets and followed him." Thankfully, Matthew uses the plural form of the word for brothers, which can mean both men and women. I've known some really wonderful lady anglers in my day—fishers of fish—and fishers of souls.

No matter what type of sport or activity you participate in, it always helps to have some education about that activity and what might be involved. Similarly, before someone can tell someone else about the hope that comes from a right relationship with Jesus Christ, they need to know what all is involved in helping others with their faith journey. In the pages ahead, I'll share some of the things that helped me with fishing and how that can relate to sharing our faith. From the training and patience involved, to the kinds of lures and the fish themselves. So, grab your favorite fishing hat, find a cozy, comfortable spot, and read on ahead. We're about to head to the lake because the fish are biting, and the water looks great!

The Training

My dad initially taught me a lot about fishing growing up. How to tie a knot when putting on a new lure and how to reel in the line. Depending on the lure, you may reel in the line fast, or reel it in intermittently. If you were fishing with real worms or grasshoppers (my favorite), you often did well with a cork and just let the bait bob in the water (or hang suspended from that cork). When the cork went under, you knew that a fish was either nibbling on your bait or taking off with it! When you knew the fish was hooked, the challenge to get that fish ashore began.

But the person I probably learned the most from was my cousin Dick. Cousin Dick was the best fisherman I knew. He had a small boat with oars, in which he would take me out whenever we went fishing. Once out on the water, he would begin teaching me the secrets of fishing. He knew about muddy water after a rain to rubbing the shaft of your fishing pole against your nose or behind the ear to get some oils that would prohibit your fishing pole from getting stuck together when it came time to take it apart. He knew about the hazards of the sun casting your shadow on the water, as well as why one bait was better than another. Cousin Dick was one of those anglers who had all his favorite lures stuck in his hat and he loved spending time on the lake, along with the tranquility that came with fishing. I'm sure he enjoyed the fish as well, but oftentimes he would just turn them loose.

Cousin Dick also showed me the different styles of fishing. There were cane poles, spin casting rods and fly-fishing rods. He could really work that fly rod and land a fly lure in the most difficult places. He was a master fisherman if I ever saw one. When cousin Dick and I would head to the lake, I always enjoyed just visiting and hearing the stories he had to tell. He had been a Marine in days gone by and we just seemed to be drawn to each other. After my military days we had an even closer relationship along with more respect for one another. But when cousin Dick took me fishing and the actual fishing time came around, there was no talking—only whispering was permitted because fish can hear you talking too!

So how does that relate to evangelism? Well, sharing one's faith can be a scary ordeal, and that's why I'm a big fan of sharing your testimony in a conversation style of evangelism. No one can take away what God has done in your life. And like fishing, it's nice to go with someone else so that you can not only enjoy each other's company, but also encourage one another as you step out in faith. Having a friend with you gives you twice the opportunity to answer questions from others. If you don't have the answer, perhaps your friend does. If you are with someone who has more experience than you, they can become a great mentor to you! Truly, mentoring and training by others helps give us additional tips and insights on methods that work and others that may be more ineffective or offensive in nature. Just like I learned how to fish initially from my dad, I learned even more from my cousin Dick. So, take advantage of opportunities to hear how other people are sharing their faith and pray whether God may want you to try something different. Most importantly, don't be too shocked when God wants to use you as a mentor to someone else who is beginning to step out and have faith conversations with others.

Additionally, just like anglers may switch lures frequently to see what is attracting fish, we need to find out the issues that people are dealing with so that we can have a point of contact or interest when praying about conversations that we can have with others. If someone is fishing for catfish, they probably will not use a lure that stays close to the surface because catfish like to hang out on the bottom where it's nice and cool. They also will use a bait that catfish love, but most fish won't touch—like liver or some other nasty-smelling bait. It is true, not all bait smells good to us, but it may be the recipe God uses to attract others to him. Not everyone cares about fishing, but some people really care about having a job, commuting safely to work, financial security, making a difference, sports, taking care of their families, raising children, and getting free of addictions just to name a few. What can you talk about that might eventually lead to a conversation about the most critical issue imaginable—where someone will spend eternity?

The Patience

Sitting on the shoreline of a lake watching a bobber that doesn't move is not the most exciting way to spend an early morning or late afternoon. That is why patience is such an important requirement when it comes to fishing or sharing our faith. I think it is also why so many lures today are designed to be cast and then reeled in at various speeds. Even old-timers would get bored if all they had to do was watch a bobber! Michael Green states an obvious truth, "most people are brought to faith through the loving persistence and friendship of someone close to them."[104] In an age when we can easily have instant gratification and possessions, fishing—and evangelism—take old fashion time and lots of patience.

Fish are pretty smart creatures. Many of them will ignore your hook, bait, or lure because they have seen this thing before and watched as their family or friends were hauled out of the water! Others will try to nibble at the bait to see if they can get something good for no commitment on their part. Still others, will run away whenever they see anything that looks like a hook, bait, or lure because of the stories they might have heard from others, or negative past experiences they have endured. That sounds a lot like people too, doesn't it? There are some people who will just ignore your best efforts, while others nibble around to make you feel good. Still others, just run whenever they see someone with a Bible.

In David Kinnaman's *You Lost Me: Why Young Christians Are Leaving the Church...and Rethinking Faith*, he shares how the prodigals—those who have left the church—have been hurt deeply. He shares that when we encounter those kinds of people (fish) we need to "respond with patience and compassion that the father in Jesus's parable displayed."[105] Many of our faith conversations will be with those who have been hurt by other people in the church. When we encounter those who have been hurt, it's time to listen with a sincere attitude—and perhaps a compassionate ear as well.

That is why prayer is so important in our work as witnesses for Christ. Tim Keller states: "The basic purpose of prayer is not to

---

104 Michael Green, *Sharing Your Faith With Family and Friends* (Grand Rapids, MI: Baker, 2005), 2.

105 Kinnaman, *You Lost Me: Why Young Christians Are Leaving Church...and Rethinking Faith*, 67.

bend God's will to mine but to mold my will into his." [106] When we strive to follow in the footsteps of Jesus, we can't help but please our heavenly Father and bring him glory. It may seem like it is not going well here on earth, but the angels are rejoicing that you made the decision to step out in faith and tell someone about the goodness of God, pray with someone who is hurting, or a multitude of other things we can do to bring glory to God and show the power of the Gospel in word and deed. That's why prayer is so important, because it will sow the seeds of kindness and faith.

Seeking God in prayer will also help align our attitudes to a Kingdom mentality instead of a selfish one. The purpose of any evangelism is to bring glory to God—not ourselves. As Robert Lee and Sara King share: "Almost nothing important gets done by just one person, especially by people in leadership roles. A leader needs patience with others and has to be comfortable with 'political' problems and with sharing or giving away credit." [107] You may think, "Well, I'm not a leader!" But the reality is—you can either lead someone to Jesus or away from Him. Every Holy Spirit-filled believer of Christ is a leader.

Patience is a real key in fishing and faith conversations too, because I've noticed that fish and people are pretty independent. People—and fish—apparently like to do things their own way. You never see another fish dragging their friends, family, or neighbors around the pond, do you? We all love to be in control! "So many of people's problems come from trying to control things outside of

---

106 Timothy Keller, *Encounters With Jesus: Unexpected Answers To Life's Biggest Questions* (New York: Dutton, 2013), 167.

107 Lee, Robert J. and Sara N. King. *Discovering the Leader in You: A Guide to Realizing Your Personal Leadership Potential*, (San Francisco: Jossey-Bass, 2001), 81.

their control, and when they try, they lose control of themselves."[108] That's why it is so important to do our best to be led of the Holy Spirit and then leave the results up to God. He alone is the ultimate judge and changer of hearts. Henry Cloud and John Townsend also shared an interesting truth about our independence and passion for control:

When Adam and Eve ate from the tree, they moved away from God and tried to gain life apart from him. They were trying to become like him, to possess god-hood for themselves and gain life outside of their relationship with God.[109]

Often our problems come when we try to exercise our free will to raise up our own gods and abilities separate from God and his direction. We try to become our own god instead of total abandonment to God alone. Ironically, the same is true in fishing. You cannot control a fish and make them swallow your bait. You just have to toss out the right bait and wait for nature to take its course. If the bait is appealing enough and your patience holds out, they will come!

The need for patience becomes a most obvious asset when confrontations arise. Since confrontation may be a very real part of a witnessing experience for you, knowing how to act in these situations can be very helpful to us all. Henry Cloud and John Townsend share a humorous but valid truth: "If you have a resistant person in your life, the number one stance you will need to adopt to learn how to deal with her is this: *Stop being surprised that she does*

---

108 Henry Cloud and John Townsend, *How People Grow: what the bible reveals personal growth* (Grand Rapids: Zondervan, 2001), 32.

109 Cloud and Townsend, *How People Grow*, 34.

not welcome the truth.[110] Realizing that some people just do not want to hear the truth, even when you share it with patience in an attitude of love and grace, helps us prepare for less-than-favorable scenarios when we have tried our best but seemingly had no success. That's why we must remember to lean on the leading of the Holy Spirit—especially when a situation gets confrontational.

We must also remember that it's a journey. We did not instantly exercise faith in Jesus Christ and the words of Scripture when conversing with others, so why would someone else do that? This is the most important decision that anyone can ever make, so we cannot expect anyone to make a decision that will affect the rest of their life in an instant.

Just like the story that Jesus shared in Luke 15:3-7, when a sheep was lost, the shepherd left the ninety-nine that were not lost in an open field and sought out the one that was lost. The Scripture tells us in verse six, that when that shepherd found the sheep, he put it on his shoulders and carried it back to where the rest of the sheep were located. If the sheep was lost and the shepherd had to leave his herd to go find this sheep, then it stands to reason, that it might have taken a little bit of time to bring that sheep back. The lost sheep wasn't just right around the corner—that wouldn't be lost. So, we must understand that instant decisions are not a normal progression unless you are the last link in a long chain of divine encounters for this person. The reality is that it takes a respectable period of time before we can help walk someone who is lost back to the fold where the rest of the sheep are located. They may have lots and lots of questions—some of which we may not have answers to right away. So be patient and rejoice that God has used you to sow some seeds of hope into a life that needs to join or rejoin the family of God one step at a time.

---

110 Henry Cloud and John Townsend, *Boundaries Face to Face* (Grand Rapids, MI: Zondervan, 2003), 151.

The Lure

When I was a kid, we mainly used "live bait" for fishing. That meant we either dug up some worms, caught grasshoppers and put them on a hook, or used liver if we were fishing for catfish. That hook was usually attached to what we called a bobber—something that floated or "bobbed" on top of the water—which in turn was attached to the fishing line tied to the end of a cane pole. It wasn't fancy, but it worked.

Today, I have noticed we have an incredible variety of fishing accessories. One sports store boasts over three hundred different types of fishing rods: deep sea, spinner rods, spin casting, and fly-fishing rods. Old fashion live bait is still used in many areas, but now we also have literally thousands of different kinds of fishing lures that fall into seven basic categories. There are jigs, spinners, spoons, soft plastic baits (worms and such), plugs, spinnerbaits/buzz baits, and flies for those fly-fishing enthusiasts.

An angler will use the best lure or bait that he or she can in order to find what the fish are hungry for that day. They don't try to shove the bait down a fish's throat if you will. They try to find what the fish are hungry for and use that type of lure to catch the most fish. They will also change up their technique or location since fish move around a lot. If you knew that a certain bait would catch the biggest fish in the lake, you would use that bait! With evangelism, I've seen people use free water stands, free nail painting, free yard work, and adopting schools to open opportunities for faith conversations just by meeting a need in the community. So, ask yourself, what needs do the people in my neighborhood or my community have that I could meet? When people see that you care enough to actually help supply a need where you live, you begin to build trusted relationships— and those can often lead to faith conversations.

Having a wide assortment of fishing lures ensures that you will have something the fish are hungry for when you are spending hours out on the water. So too, there are so many differing styles of evangelism or methods of sharing one's faith that we don't really need to be offensive! Hebrews 4:12 tells us: "For the word of God is living and active, sharper than any two-edged sword, piercing to the division of soul and spirit, of joints and marrow, and discerning the thoughts and intentions of the heart." With such a powerful tool as the Word of God, we can let God do whatever is necessary in a person's life by just sharing His Word.

Not everyone loves confrontational evangelism, but there are times when that might be appropriate—like the time a drunk person was brought to my home church. It was an evening service that we were attending, since our schedule happened to be free of ministry that evening. We were in the middle of the worship service and I was focusing on the worship with my eyes closed, when someone touched my shoulder. I looked up and a dear friend in the church asked me to come with him for some help with a person they had with them. I wasn't sure what to expect, but I followed him over to where they were standing along the side of the sanctuary. He told me that they found this man lying face down on the side of the road and had gotten him up and brought him to church. I introduced myself to the man and asked him name—while simultaneously noticing the alcohol on his breath.

I knew this would not be a case where talking about my faith would just come up over coffee. The Holy Spirit seemed to reveal to me that I needed to get right to the point with this gentleman. So, I just asked him, "How's your relationship with God?"

He said, "Well, I don't know."

I said, "You need to get things right with the Lord. You need to ask Jesus Christ into your heart to have leadership and Lordship of your life."

He said, "I know. I just need to get myself cleaned up first."

I replied to his excuse and said, "You can't get cleaned up enough to get right with God. He died on a cross for you and that forgiveness is free. Would you like that right now?"

He said, "Yes."

So, I prayed for him right then and there. Thankfully, the Holy Spirit seemed to really give me a boost of faith when I was talking to this gentleman. I know that the boldness of that conversation did not come from me alone, but through the presence of the Holy Spirit in that situation.

You might say, "Well, he was intoxicated and probably did not really get saved." My answer to that is I'm not the judge. I just tried to follow the prompting of the Holy Spirit and speak candidly with this man about getting his life right with God. That was the "bait" I used if you'll excuse the analogy. Only God knows what was going on inside this man's heart.

True anglers have a feel for what might work and what might not work. Their years of experience only make them better about discerning what might be the best lure in that situation. Likewise, sharing your faith with others will get easier over time as well, although you may always have some anxiety when you are getting ready to take that first step. Thankfully, the Christian has an added benefit that regular anglers don't have. We have a divine Helper in the Holy Spirit, who loves to help us gain a sensitivity to His leading and show us the proper approach with different people, and situations, if we will only listen to Him.

The Hook

Whenever you are fishing with a lure or fresh bait, you have to be mindful of the hook. Without a hook, the fish would just swallow the lure or bait and then you would pull it right back out! You would be hard pressed to catch a fish without a hook. The hook is made with a barb or series of barbs on the end of the hook to keep it from slipping out once the hook has been swallowed. If you ever get the hook so deep in your skin that the barbs are caught too, you usually have to push the hook through the skin and cut off the barb with some wire cutters—not a happy event in anyone's life.

That reminds me of the time my younger brother got mad at me. When I was about twelve or thirteen, I was swimming with some of my siblings in the creek not far from our house. My younger brother thought that was a good time to go fishing and was not happy that we were swimming in his fishing spot. I'm not sure what prompted his actions, but at one point he took a swipe at me with his fishing rod. He was fishing with those plastic worms that normally have three hooks in them. When he swung that fishing pole, all three hooks stuck in my back! He dropped the pole and headed for the house, because he knew I was pretty mad at that point. Thankfully, the barbs had not gone deep enough to stick, and my sister was able to pull the hooks out. All that to say, manmade hooks hurt!

In evangelism, whenever we strive to make converts by manipulation and other manmade methods of coercion, more often than not the conversion experience is not a true conversion experience. The wonderful thing about God's spiritual hooks is that they do not hurt. As a matter of fact, God's hook has such an appeal that we often cannot resist his invitation. The Word of God is a living Word and we need only to let it loose to see what God can do. The Scriptures contain the right words and the right hook that will capture people's attention and stir up a desire for a restored relationship with Christ.

As Jesus said in John 12:32, "And I, when I am lifted up from the earth, will draw all people to myself." There is just something about Jesus Christ that hooks a person or catches someone's attention. A hook can be used in fishing, to hang something on a wall, or something crafted to catch people's attention. Songs have a hook, or catchy lyric, that seems to stick in your head. Some forms of literature have a hook that seems so simple, yet stays with you whenever you hear a certain word or story. The Word of God contains that kind of hook—something that draws us closer to this person called Jesus Christ. Sometimes, the most attractive thing about Christianity is the Christlike action by one of His followers.

The Fish

According to the California Academy of Sciences' Catalog of Fishes, "the number of valid species of fishes is 34,815."[111] Just thinking about that many fish makes my head hurt, but you can just bet that they do not all eat the same thing. They all have differing dispositions and go through their life cycles in unique ways.

Fish are like humans in many ways. They like to eat and enjoy the shade when it's hot. That is why the biggest fish seem to be around piers or fallen trees, where the best shade and food can be found. Fish are also wary of anything out of the ordinary. When I was young, one of the first things I learned from my cousin Dick, was to keep from standing where the sun was behind you because that position would cast your shadow on the water. If you can see your shadow, a fish can too. Likewise, talking about any subject that stirs up anxiety can cause other people to flee—like talking about a person's faith! Sometimes, we need to be direct in talking about the Gospel, while at other times a conversational approach works best. Regardless of the method, all people—and fish—are different, so we need to be sensitive to the leading of the Holy Spirit to guide us in using the right approach.

---

111 http://researcharchive.calacademy.org/research/ichthyology/catalog/ SpeciesByFamily.asp. Accessed July 27, 2018.

When you think about all the kids in your school growing up, you may remember that there were a lot of different personalities. Some were the athletic crowd, some were the cheerleading and popular crowd, some were the really smart, nerdy crowd, and some just did not care. Every single one of us is different—thank goodness—and that means many of us go through different life experiences. Because we are all unique, we have differing interests and skills in which we seem gifted. We even have different tastes! Some people love Italian food, others Tex-Mex, and still others enjoy German, Polish, Indian, or a plethora of other different cultural foods.

If there are so many people who enjoy so many different kinds of food, don't you think that those same people might also value different approaches to conversations—especially ones that are sensitive in nature. That is why one style of outreach or evangelism—our bait and lure if you will—will never reach everyone. When I worked as a mechanic, I sometimes needed special tools to fix certain problems. Those special tools gave me access to areas that would have taken me a lot longer to fix otherwise. So too, we have different approaches to evangelism because sometimes God wants to use a very unique way to reach a certain group of people.

We talk about relational, or friendship, evangelism that works at building a trusted relationship or friendship over time so that we can share about sensitive issues like faith and religion. We have confrontational evangelism when we just need to be a little more direct in our approach, like when we are in an emergency situation or someone has just been confronted with a life-changing experience. Even ministry in some foreign countries is expected to be more confrontational because you could be killed for what you believe or say.

Intellectual evangelism is more of an apologetic approach, or defense, of the Gospel. This is where folks who are gifted in the academic arena use logical reasoning, facts, and historical proofs to substantiate Scripture. They love engaging in debates on college campuses or anywhere else for that matter—just for an opportunity to defend the truths of Scripture.

We make up other names for these types of evangelism, like conversational evangelism, where topics of Gospel presentation strategically come up. Or questioning evangelism, wherein strategic questions are asked to help direct a conversation to spiritual aspects of life that can be discussed. The true motive isn't deception, it is a heart-felt desire to share the wonderful truths of Scripture with those who do not know Jesus—and help them escape the judgment to come.

So, use various baits to see what works and what does not. Don't be discouraged and quit when something doesn't work—just change tactics—or your lure. Continue learning different ways to share the hope that is within you and admit mistakes when you make them. People are a lot more patient when they see that those who are trying to share their faith are doing so out of a heart of love and compassion for them—not just success over gaining another convert.

Help Can Be Nice

When I was around five or six years old, dad took us all fishing. I was given liver that Dad used to bait my hook for some catfish. I had a bobber that floated on top of the water to keep my bait off the lake bottom and let me see when a fish had swallowed my liver. I remember being on my knees holding my fishing rod while Dad went off around the lake trying to help my other brothers and sisters. I have no recollection of what I was thinking while kneeling by the water's edge, but I distinctly remember when something grabbed my bait and tried to take off.

I was holding on for dear life—clutching that fishing pole with every bit of strength I could muster—and yelling for my dad to come help me. The fish was apparently so big (no fooling) that it was starting to slowly drag me into the water. The fact that I was kneeling on a somewhat muddy bank did not help matters much either. For some reason, I could not stand up, but I was determined not to let go of that fishing pole! When my dad finally came around the lake where I was kneeling—walking instead of running like I wanted him to—he had to beach that catfish. He said that was the biggest one he had ever caught in that lake, which made me feel pretty good in front of my brothers and sisters!

I needed some help getting my catfish to shore that day, and sometimes we need some spiritual help in our evangelism or outreach efforts to harvest the fruit that God has given us. Jesus knew the challenges His disciples would face in sharing the Gospel message, and He took steps to help them as well. At the end of Luke chapter 9, Jesus begins to share with his disciples about the cost of following Him. Then, in chapter 10 verse 1, Luke tells us that Jesus "appointed seventy-two others and sent them on ahead of him, two by two, into every town and place where he himself was about to go." In Mark 6:7, we're told that Jesus "called the twelve and began to send them out two by two, and gave them authority over the unclean spirits." In Matthew chapter 18, Jesus shares about the importance of accountability, and then in verse 19 says, "Again I say to you, if two of you agree on earth about anything they ask, it will be done for them by my Father in heaven." There was a reason Jesus sent His disciples out in twos—accountability, encouragement, and the power of agreement.

Sometimes, like with fishing, we enjoy being by ourselves. But there are times, when fishing for really big fish or large numbers of fish, that you need a team! Just like when I caught that huge catfish and needed help from my dad to get that fish to shore, there are times when we need help in our evangelism efforts. There are plenty of folks who are not interested in hearing about the hope that is within us, but there are some standing at the precipice of eternity and God is counting on you and me to listen to that still, small, voice of God and obey His nudging. He longs for us to be "instant in season" (2 Timothy 4:2 KJV), to share a word of hope and encouragement with someone who needs to know that God really does love and care about them. I love how the Message Bible phrases 2 Timothy 4:1-2,

> I can't impress this on you too strongly. God is looking over your shoulder. Christ himself is the Judge, with the final say on everyone, living and dead. He is about to break into the open with his rule, so proclaim the Message with intensity; keep on your watch. Challenge, warn, and urge your people. Don't ever quit. Just keep it simple.

Keeping it simple, and getting help when needed, are keys to effective evangelism and outreach efforts, which helps eliminate frustrations that can arise when we make something more complex than needed.

You Just Might Be Blessed

The Lord taught me a valuable lesson when I was helping with a community outreach in the New Orleans area one year during Mardi Gras. Our group had come together in a particular neighborhood to host a clothing give-away, provide some worship music, and free lunch. We cooked hamburgers and hotdogs for the meal and prior to that our teams split up to go door-to-door and hand out flyers, inviting folks to come enjoy the free event in their neighborhood.

After a while, for some reason, I took off by myself to see if I could find some additional folks to join us for the free food, clothing giveaway, and time of worship. At one home, I met Monroe, who had a scar over the top of his head—from one ear to the other. He had some speech issues, but after I asked him if there was anything

I could pray with him about, he began to bless me. He told me how he watched a certain television preacher every morning, read his Bible and prayed for those in his neighborhood.

Monroe began to pray for me, and I couldn't help but weep as his passionate prayer seemed to elicit something from heaven. I stood there with this giant of a man, who many would say needed help, and received something that money could not buy. I was overwhelmed by the presence of God that day—all while trying to be the hands and feet of Jesus extended. We chatted a bit more afterwards and I invited him to the outreach. While I was walking back to the outreach area, the Holy Spirit seemed to say to me, "See, you thought you came out here to minister to these people, but I used them to minister to you." The Lord reminded me that He was just looking for a willing vessel—one that He could use—and bless at the most unexpected time.

Casting for Heavenly Treasures

Casting a fishing rod is an art, plain and simple. Just like playing sports, there are tips and tricks to getting the lure where it needs to go. In basketball, you have to know when to release the ball when shooting for a basket. When you play baseball, you have to know when to release the ball when you are throwing it to someone else or pitching to a batter. As the quarterback on a football team, you must know when to release the ball in order for it to go to its intended receiver. So too, in fishing the cast is one of the most important techniques that a person has to learn. It helps you get the lure, or bait, where it needs to go in order to potentially catch a fish.

Even when you know the art of casting, it takes a lot of practice to master a particular technique. And as with any technique, you will find that you like some more than others, and find some easier to perform than others. When I was young, I only had a cane pole with a line, a bobber that floated on top of the water, and live bait—usually worms or grasshoppers. Casting was pretty simple. You just plopped your line out in the water and waited until that bobber began to bob. Now, with all the different types of fishing rods the art of casting has evolved.

In doing some brief studying, I discovered there are six basic casting rod techniques that all have one goal in mind—getting the lure or bait out to where the fish are hanging out. For beginners, there is the overhead cast, the sidearm cast (less splash) and the drop cast, which is much like the good old days of cane pole fishing. For more advanced anglers there is the pitch, the flip, and the skip. All of these have particular circumstances that encourage their usage. The reality is that an angler is going to use whatever technique is needed, whether there is a name for it or not, in order to place that bait where a fish can get it.

The same analogy of casting can be used when witnessing or sharing with someone else the wonderful things God has done in your life through faith conversations. I can't tell you how many times I've heard someone say, "Evangelism is just not my gift." But I have noticed that almost everyone can talk, which means that every single Christian can say something good about their faith if it came up in a conversation.

Honestly, I think we Christians beat ourselves up too much. And since we don't feel like we measure up to our own individual standards of what we think an "evangelist" for Jesus Christ looks like, we just give up and don't do anything. Evangelist Luis Palau has shared on more than one occasion that evangelism "is not an option" for those who called themselves Christians. It should actually be a part of our daily lives. God did not mean for sharing our faith to be difficult. Have people suffered and been persecuted for their faith? You bet. In the Western world we don't see that often, but it does still happen in many parts of the world.

That said, there are many times when God seems to take us outside of our comfort zone in order to share a timely word with someone who is desperately seeking answers to life's problems. It literally feels like the scariest thing on earth to actually say something positive about your faith journey with another person who we fear may not be receptive. However, Dr. George G. Hunter III makes a valid point about this:

> People, after all, are more likely to sense the revelation being mediated through us when they perceive our discomfort; and when they sense that we care about them enough to experience discomfort while helping them, they are more likely to respond.[112]

So, perhaps the question we should ask ourselves is: "Do I love this person enough to offer some hope through the sharing of God's goodness in my life?" I pray you'll answer yes to that question and ask God for more opportunities to speak about Him to those you love.

Using Your Own Artform

I can readily admit that sharing one's faith seems like an artform. Some people seem to always have a ready answer and are quick to share their faith in the most embarrassing situations. Those folks become energized by confrontational witnessing encounters. However, that does not seem to be the normal artform most Christians prefer.

---

112 George G. Hunter III, *The Apostolic Congregation: Church Growth Reconceived for A New Generation* (Nashville, TN: Abingdon, 2009), 122.

Just like casting, there are artforms to sharing one's faith that are more appealing to you than other techniques. Just because you abhor one technique of evangelism, don't disregard them all. Some Christians thoroughly enjoy an articulated, intelligent debate on the facts of Christianity. If that's you, welcome to a more intellectual approach to sharing your faith. Some Christians seem gifted at asking just the right questions at the right time—a more inquisitive approach. Asking questions allows non-believers to discern for themselves why Christianity might be a legitimate faith path for them to consider.

Most Christians love having fellowship with friends and family and would be more than happy to answer a serious question about Christianity if they were asked. I might add, it is okay to tell someone you don't know the answer, but you'll do some research and get back with them! We don't need to feel like we must be the answer-man or -woman before we can engage in a conversation about faith issues— that's just not a reasonable expectation. We need to let people know that we struggle just like everyone else, but we have an incredible advocate on our side. The Bible speaks to every area of life and we don't need to keep that a secret.

Listening also seems to go a long way to making an impact on people and making room for Gospel seeds to be sown when an opportunity avails itself. As a Christian, just our presence, or perhaps the Holy Spirit's presence in us, can cause others to share certain challenges in their lives. As I shared earlier, evangelism can be as simple as asking, "Have you been praying about that?" when a friend talks about difficult decisions or issues in their life. It's a very innocent question that will not only help you see where they are spiritually, but also open an opportunity to respond in a sincere way, like: "I'm so sorry to hear that. I'll be praying specifically about that. Do you mind if I add that to our church's prayer list?" If they hesitate, just say that's okay, but that you'll be keeping them in prayer whether they like it or not because they are your friend!

There are so many ways to show and convey our faith to others that the number of "techniques" are limitless. You just need to ask the Holy Spirit what He wants you to say in those situations. Part of sharing our faith is praying for opportunities and then waiting on the Holy Spirit to guide our steps, techniques, and words to share. You can do this! It simply involves starting conversations wherein there is a trusted comfort level that allows for sharing seeds about our faith journey and how it could help someone else.

So, grab your spiritual fishing rod and start casting—okay, I'm just kidding—but the reality is that you are already equipped with the needed techniques if you believe in Jesus Christ and have asked Him to be the Lord and Leader of your life. With just a few Scriptures and a heart that truly cares about your friends, family, and acquaintances, you can begin having spiritual chats. These are merely discussions that afford opportunities for you to sow seeds of faith into your conversation—and change a person's life for eternity.

That Awful Moss

Moss was one of the most frustrating challenges about fishing when I was growing up. If you have never been fishing, imagine a smooth-as-glass lake, but it appears that there is something growing along the shoreline as you get closer to the water's edge. It is dark, green, and thick. Whenever you cast out your line and start reeling in the line with your lure on the end, everything is fine until you get close to shore. Then, all of a sudden, it seems like your lure catches a bit wad of green mush—moss! It reminded me of the time I caught a snapping turtle. I felt like I had hooked a sunken log and was pulling in buried treasure—but I was sadly mistaken! Thankfully, the snapping turtle snapped my line before he got to shore. Although there are some who take great delight in snapping turtle delicacies, for me, moss falls right in the same category as sunken logs, ticks, and chiggers.

Moss comes in many forms, with the most recognizable form in seaweed for many who never grew up in a rural setting. If you have ever gone to the beach, you may have seen some seaweed that washed upon the shore at some point. Moss is a lot like that since it is a green vegetation that grows in the non-saltwater reservoirs like lakes, ponds, creeks, and such.

When I was little, I always thought moss looked a lot like cooked spinach or greens—which may have been the cause of my apprehension with that wonderful vegetable early on in life. Thankfully, there is quite a difference between the smell of moss and cooked spinach, which I've grown to love over the years. Now, I look forward to a heaping, helping of cooked spinach, or any of the greens' family (mustard, poke, and turnip), while I continue to try and avoid moss whenever possible. Ha! There is just something about lake water and fish-smelling moss that is off-putting to me for some reason.

The most challenging thing about moss is that it can be extremely hard to get off your lure, which is dangerous for a youngster. We have no patience for such tedious chores like cleaning moss out of lures—we just want to catch fish! That moss can be slimy and clings with a tenacity to your lure that is similar to trying to get a pork chop away from a bull dog—it's not possible. Moss will not fall off or fling off—you have to pull every bit off of your lure.

The reason for cleaning moss off of a lure stems from the fact that fish know all about moss. As a matter of fact, they love it! They can hide in it and feed on other critters that hide in it. I'm sure they love to play numerous hid- and-seek games with other fish in their moss haven. I mean, what else is there to do on a lazy Sunday afternoon?

One thing is certain, fish are not about to be tricked into eating a worm or lure that has moss on it. They know what a normal worm, bug, fly, or insect looks like. As a kid, I would try to sling that moss off of my plastic worm by slamming it on the ground to get most of the moss off. I was successful in part, but a little moss always remained, and I could never catch a fish with moss still on my lure. So, without fail, I would have to pick off every speck of moss if I wanted even the slightest chance at catching a fish at all.

In a Christian's life, moss is a lot like sin. When we try to share our faith with others and our relationship with God is not right, the moss in our lives puts a barrier between the goodness of the Gospel and those who need it. After twenty years in ministry, I have seen a lot that isn't God in the Church. But the reality is that we're all just humans in a fallen world trying our best to live for Christ. The Scriptures tell us that this world isn't our eternal home (1 Peter 2:11-12), and when we get to that heavenly home, we'll be perfect. But until then, we'll struggle a bit trying to live a godly life.

That doesn't give us an excuse to do whatever we want on this side of heaven, but it is a challenge for us all to be aware that our actions speak louder than our words. As a matter of fact, I've done a lot of apologizing to people who have been hurt by the Church and its people. We are not perfect, but if we're not careful, the moss of sin in our own lives can hinder our ability to share the amazing story of what God has done in our lives!

The Scriptures tell us that we all need to pick up our cross daily (Luke 9:23), so no one should be pointing fingers, but it is an exhortation for us all to work at removing that awful moss in our lives on a daily basis. God is just waiting to use your story to speak into the life of someone needing to hear about the transforming power of a relationship with Christ. Nobody can take your story away from you and I hope you're as excited about sharing it as I am!

YOUR ASSIGNMENT

1. Set some time aside each day to ask God to reveal any moss (sin) that may be creeping into your life. That may be during your morning commute to work on the train, bus, metro, or other mode of transportation.

2. Think about your "fishing" strengths. What areas of your life have you seen God do some amazing things that you could share if it came up in conversation? What questions could you ask a friend that might lead the conversation to these areas of discussion?

3. Think through the different styles of evangelism (casting) and mentally list one or two of your stronger styles—confrontational, intellectual, relational, etc.

4. List some activities or situations where these evangelism styles could "naturally" come into play. I love to "play to my strengths" as the saying goes, but sometimes God really takes me out of my comfort zone. What would be your most uncomfortable encounter? Why? It's good to have an answer for not doing certain things when people try to manipulate us into certain evangelism molds.

5. Keep a list of the fish that God has allowed you to have a part in reeling into His harvest. We should celebrate when someone comes to know the Lord…I hope you do!

MY PRAYER LIST

I'm praying for (those individuals God has put in your life who may not have a right relationship with God yet, or people for whom God has burdened you to pray):

_____

_____

_____

_____

_____

_____

_____

_____

_____

_____

_____

_____

CHAPTER 8

RELAY

L.E.A.**R**.N. Evangelism means to:

RELAY – Relay some aspect of your faith journey that includes the Gospel message.

There is no single, correct way to share your faith, but at some point, you need to relay how a relationship with Jesus Christ has impacted your life. You should consider sharing a combination of God's Word and your testimony, or the testimony of someone you know if your experiences don't relate to the person you are talking to. Since one of your assignments in chapter six was to write out your testimony (with additional insights in chapter ten), you are now equipped to tell others what God has done in your life with clarity. In listening and asking a question or two, you will usually discover an opportunity to share your testimony—what God has done in your life (1 Peter 3:15). You may even feel inclined to ask permission to share what God's done for you. No one can dispute your testimony, so make sure you write it down and know it by heart. Using Scripture phrased as questions ("Did you know that God's Word—the Bible - says in…") helps others see God's plan and sincere love for them and their loved ones.

SCRIPTURES

Some Scriptures (ESV) to share might include:
— Romans 3:23, *For all have sinned and fall short of the glory of God.* (ESV)
  - Billy Graham once said, "Sin is any thought or action that falls short of God's will." We all have a sinful nature.
— 1 John 5:17 says that: "All unrighteousness is sin."
  - You can't save yourself…and no one else can save you except Jesus Christ. How?
— Romans 5:8, …*but God shows his love for us in that while we were still sinners, Christ died for us."*
— Rom 6:23, *For the wages of sin is death, but the free gift of God is eternal life in Christ Jesus our Lord.*
  - Jesus Christ willingly paid a price for our sins because He was the only one who could.
— John 3:16, *For God so loved the world, that he gave his only Son, that whoever believes in him should not perish but have everlasting life.*
  - God loves you so much that He allowed His son to die in your place. We didn't deserve this free gift of salvation…
— 2 Corinthians 5:17, *Therefore, if anyone is in Christ, he is a new creation. The old has passed away; Behold, the new has come.*
  - Would you like to experience that kind of newness of life?
— Romans 10:13, "*For everyone who calls on the name of the Lord will be saved.'"*
  - When you ask Jesus to forgive you of sin and ask Him to have Lordship and leadership of your life, then you are saved! That's called salvation and only God can provide that—it cannot be earned!

WHAT DOES IT MEAN TO "BE SAVED?"

Being *SAVED* is an expression that even Christians find difficult to define. While here on earth, being saved means we have asked God to forgive us of our wrongdoings and to have leadership of our lives. In doing so, we have an advocate or helper in Jesus Christ, who is interceding for us and who has sent the Holy Spirit to help us here on earth. Being *SAVED* also means that when we die, we will spend eternity in the presence of God. The Scripture states that "we shall all stand before the judgment seat of Christ" (Romans 14:10). Being saved involves accepting God's forgiveness for our sins through the work of Jesus Christ on the cross and inviting Jesus Christ to have Lordship and leadership of our lives (John 14:6). Then, we will avoid, or be *SAVED* from, the eternal damnation or separation from God that comes to those who reject Christ. Remember Romans 6:23 states that the "wages of sin is death." That is a spiritual death which causes a separation from God. Only through Christ's sacrifice on the cross is there forgiveness and the restoring of a right relationship with God.

After sharing your testimony and Scripture is a great time to ask again if you haven't already, "Have you ever had an experience with Jesus Christ like that?" If they answer "No," you can ask, "Would you like to?" If they avoid the question or get defensive don't worry, just move on and let them know that God loves them and just seemed to nudge you to talk with them about their faith journey. However, if they say "Yes," you can share a small prayer with them and 2 Corinthians 5:17. The exact words of the prayer are not all that important—what matters is the intent of the heart.

Prayer For Salvation

Dear Jesus, here I am. I'm not perfect; I am a sinner. I ask you to come into my heart and forgive me of my sins. Please be the Lord of my life; and lead me all the days of my life. In Jesus' name, Amen.

CHRIST IN ACTION

Some of Christ's choicest servants are servants indeed. What do I mean by that? I mean that many faithful followers of Jesus Christ are extremely shy about starting extemporaneous conversations with people they do not even know. That is why servant evangelism arises as such a powerful avenue for sharing the Gospel. Many people who would never even think about broaching the subject of a person's faith journey would be the first in line to pay for someone's meal who stood in line behind them or in a car waiting behind them in the drive through lane at a fast food restaurant. The servant evangelist would not have to think twice, if they sensed God's gentle nudge to anonymously pay for the meal of a person sitting in a restaurant where they were dining, who looked like they could use some encouragement. They wouldn't have to ponder the appropriateness of helping an elderly person with their grocery bags or assist with an array of any other needs that presented themselves.

Why do I share these insights? Because, for too long, we have excelled at criticizing ourselves for what we have failed to do. We need to encourage one another for the little things we do for the sake of evangelism as Paul told the Thessalonians (1 Thessalonians 5:11). Instead of pointing out our evangelistic shortcomings, we need to recognize that some Christians are more gifted in confrontational approaches, while others are better suited for alternate styles of evangelism. Living a Christlike lifestyle is not a life that needs to apologize for anything. Your visual acts of Christian kindness to others will speak volumes to people. That in itself, may actually start conversations! When people catch you doing something unselfishly nice, they just may ask you why you are doing that. They may also use their smartphones to record your actions and brag about them on social media. Then, you have the perfect opportunity to share how Christ has transformed your life and that you just wanted to share some of God's love with others to let them know that God cares about them. Scattering the Gospel seed isn't always about talking. At times, "doing" speaks far louder in the hearts and minds of those in a place of struggle.

Youth groups have displayed servant evangelism by adopting classrooms and caring for elementary school playgrounds to demonstrate the love of Christ through tangible means. Parks, and other areas in the public view in your community are prime avenues to show the love of God through actions in your own city. Steve Sjogren, who wrote the excellent book, *Conspiracy of Kindness*, shares that servant evangelism is only one method of evangelism and that it doesn't always work. He shares, "And like any other approach, it simply doesn't work apart from the agency of the Holy Spirit who is the only true evangelist."[113] But as Steve points out, most people will remember feeling the love of God through an act of kindness more vividly than someone just telling them about God's love. So, don't be ashamed of how you share God's love... just the fact that you are trying to share God's love the best way you know how is a wonderful reflection upon your personal decision to do evangelism.

---

113 Steve Sjogren, *Conspiracy of Kindness*, 23.

A DEEPER LOOK AT LEADING SOMEONE TO CHRIST

Not all evangelism is created equal. As I have shared, there are numerous types or methods of evangelism. Some have broken these down into categories like: Confrontational, Questioning, Intellectual, Testimonial, Interpersonal, Relational, Conversational, Invitational, Event, and Serving. There may be numerous other method titles, but the main thing we all need to understand is that we should be ourselves. Whichever methods we tend to migrate towards is how we best communicate our own faith journey.

No matter what style we use, we must bathe the process in prayer. Mark Mittelberg stated in his *Becoming A Contagious Church* book, "If we want to be contagious Christians and to build a contagious church, prayer must be woven into the very fabric of *all* we do."[114] Since we are setting out to do God's business and follow His command to take the Gospel to all nations, then it makes sense that we need to be led by Him.

God has called us to "make disciples" and we do that by keeping a vision or focus of spreading the seed of the Gospel. In Matthew 13, Jesus tells a parable about the seed and the sower. A parable is merely a story conveying a point or overarching truth. In this parable, some seeds that were scattered by the sower fell along the roadside, some fell on stony places, some fell among thorns, and some fell on good ground. In Jesus' day, roads were often just pathways through the fields and seeds would fall upon the ground and be trampled underfoot. We are called to scatter the seed everywhere and let God worry about what happens to the seed. This parable reveals that not every seed will bear fruit, but where the seed lands is not as important as the act of continually scattering

---

114 Mark Mittelberg, *Becoming A Contagious Church: Increase the Evangelistic Temperature in Your Church*, rev. ed. (Grand Rapids, MI: Zondervan, 2007), 23.

seed. The seed is always good, and it will never run out, so feel free to sow that Gospel seed with gusto!

As I shared in an earlier chapter, when I was a young Christian, I went through the Evangelism Explosion training course. There are other similar training courses today that can act as an evangelism mentor. If we're honest with ourselves, sometimes we just need a little help in putting evangelism into practice. If you ever have the opportunity, I would encourage you to jump into a structured environment that will give you solid tools to use in sharing your faith.

Personally, I thought Evangelism Explosion was an excellent way to learn a barebones outline of helping people understand and come to the place where they could make a decision to follow Christ. It wasn't perfect, but it gave a person an understanding of the basics of the Gospel. We all have different personalities and experiences, so those things will round out the way we present the message of Jesus Christ. I want to take the basics of the Evangelism Explosion training and build on them here to help us gain some insights of what this process might look like. But first, a little background.

Evangelism Explosion

Evangelism Explosion is an evangelistic training program that was first started in 1967 at Coral Ridge Presbyterian Church in Fort Lauderdale, Florida by Dr. James Kennedy. It evolved due to the emergence of the increasingly educated layperson in the church; the monumental need to share the Gospel with an ever-increasing population, and the realization that clergy alone could not begin to accomplish this task.

The mindset of the typical layperson in the church at this time—and probably still is in large part today—held a belief that it was the minister's job to save souls and fight spiritual battles. It was apparently thought that evangelism was the work of professionally trained clergy. But Jesus gave us all the great commission in Matthew 28:18-20, which tells us to "Go ye therefore, and teach all nations…" (KJV). We all have a responsibility to share the Gospel, and Evangelism Explosion was designed to help take the fear out of doing this.

The Evangelistic Explosion level one course is a sixteen-week training program that takes the typical lay person from being timid and uncertain to a confident presenter of the Gospel. The program is separated into units that are assigned weekly, with progressive hands-on tools that tell how to present the Gospel to someone in a non-threatening way. Outlines of presentation methods, as well as relative Scriptures, are memorized in preparation for the actual presentation. Groups of three people, usually two men and one woman, are sent out. One of these three will be the leader of the group and will have experience in outreach ministry. The leader will initially start conversations and then gradually draw the other individuals into the presentation over the course of the sixteen-week period.

By the end of the sixteen weeks, the group leader will let the trainees give the entire presentation. This method of training follows a basic outline of introductions, the Gospel presentation, the commitment of the believer, and follow-up of the new convert. There are actually four levels of instruction that can be taken in the Evangelism Explosion program, and these all build onto the sixteen-week level one program.

There are some criticisms of the Evangelism Explosion program. Two of these are: the problem of getting people to commit to sixteen weeks of training, and the other is that this training just puts a canned speech in the hands of those witnessing. To say that no one will commit to sixteen weeks is a little presumptuous, for the Lord has truly given some a burden for the lost. People who are in the training have report-back meetings in which those who witness give testimonies of their experiences as well as commitments that were made for salvation. This not only encourages the new trainees but also gives them ideas to use in their own witnessing techniques. As their techniques improve, they are continually polishing their presentation so that it doesn't sound like a canned speech, no matter what the situation. Although criticisms come, churches around the world using programs like Evangelism Explosion are making a difference, and the growth in their congregations reflects it.

The need for training like Evangelism Explosion seems obvious. Most organizations train individuals in personal evangelism, and then send them into the field with no tools for hands-on application. We have all heard the expression that it's better to teach a boy how to fish than to give the boy a fish. So too, is it better to teach people how to win souls than to win souls all by yourself. The multiplication factor of one trainer training two or three other individuals, and those in turn training another two or three individuals, is unquestionably getting God's people back on the right track. Dr. Kennedy said that he was petrified at the idea of witnessing, even after taking evangelism classes for three years. He said, "It was not until someone who knew how (to witness) had taken me out into people's homes that I finally got the confidence to do it myself."[115] Training people in the church in sharing the Gospel helps give those lacking a relationship with Jesus Christ an opportunity to make a life-changing decision. A program like Evangelism Explosion is a great way to place the necessary tools into our hands.

---

115 D. James Kennedy, *Evangelism Explosion*, 3rd ed. (Wheaton, IL: Tyndale Publishing, 1983), 6.

Opening The Front Door

As you actually begin to exercise your sharing skills, there are some ideas you may want to consider. When we are trying to start spiritual conversations with others, we often need to begin in the arena of another person's secular life: their job, their responsibilities, their families, etc. We are looking for a connecting point where conversations can begin. You are also trying to build a relationship that is strong enough to allow permission—whether asked or implied—to ask more personal questions like these below. As we have mentioned before, an extremely important part of spiritual conversations is listening. "This is very important in one-on-one evangelism. You ask questions, and you actually listen to the answers. Then you appropriately apply the Gospel to their situation."[116]

- "Do you like your life right now?"
- "Are you really happy where you are?"
- "Do you ever think about spiritual issues?"
- "You look like you could use a friend."
- "What's the hardest thing you wrestle with?"

You can also talk about their church background:

- "Do you go to church anywhere?"

You can bring up something incredible that has recently happened at your church:

- "Boy, we had a great service last night!"

My favorite is sharing your testimony or a testimony of someone recently from your church:

- "What's the most amazing thing that happened in your life? For me it was…"

---

116 Greg Laurie, *Tell Someone: You Can Share the Good News*, (Nashville, TN: B&H Publishing, 2016), Kindle edition, location 927.

- **NOTE: If you haven't written down your testimony you should do it today! See more details about that in Chapter 10.**

Once you have started the conversation about faith issues and you feel the Holy Spirit leading you, ask a more inquisitive question like:

- "Have you come to a place in your spiritual life where you *know for certain* that if you were to die today you would go to heaven?"
- Make this personal by stating their name—"Mary, have you come to a place...."
- "Suppose that you were to die tonight and stand before God and he were to say to you, 'Why should I let you into my heaven?' What would you say?"
- Again, use their name to make this a personal concern of yours.
- "If something terrible happened tonight and you were in a fatal accident, do you know where you would spend eternity?"

If you are not sincerely concerned with the person's eternal resting place, please do not ask these questions. People know when you are not sincere or when you are merely going through the motions. However, if you are truly sincere when you ask these questions, those people will know that you cared enough to ask and will usually overlook the awkward nature of those questions.

If someone answers one of those last questions with, "Well, I hope so," that is a great time for us to ask, "Would you like to know for sure?" When you get "permission" you can then share God's wonderful plan with assurance that the Holy Spirit is helping you—whether you feel like it or not! Sometimes, when we feel the most anxious is when the Holy Spirit is the closest. Here are some aspects of the Gospel that you could share.

Insights Into Sharing The Gospel

So, what is this plan of salvation anyway? Well, it seems very logical to conclude that if there is an all-powerful, all-knowing, and everywhere-present Creator of the universe, He must have had a plan. As a matter of fact, the Scripture tells us in Colossians 1:16, "For by him all things were created, in heaven and on earth, visible and invisible, whether thrones or dominions or rulers or authorities—all things were created through him and for him."

People need to realize that God had an original plan for His creation. When I speak to audiences, I like to remind people that God has a great plan for their life; and if God has a great plan for their life, then it is a lot better than the plan they have for their own lives. God's a big God! I used to think that God was so big that he could not have time for the minutiae of my tiny world and its problems. But the reality is just the opposite. Because God is so big, he can know even the smallest details of your dreams that you've never shared with anyone for fear that they might not come true—that's how big your God is—a God full of grace and mercy.

Grace is an amazing word and a wonderful attribute that I need in my personal and professional relationships. I appreciate it when other people give me enough grace to make mistakes and learn from them. However, that kind of grace is usually something that I had to earn over a lengthy period of time. God's grace[117] is often defined as unmerited favor—we can't earn it or work hard enough to achieve it. In short—we don't deserve it. But God's awesome grace has given us all a great, eternal gift. The wonderful thing about a gift is that your ability to receive it is all that's required. If

---

117 A brief outline of the Gospel presentation is shown on pages 16-23 of D. James Kennedy's *Evangelism Explosion*, 3rd ed. (Wheaton, IL: Tyndale Publishing, 1983), training manual.

we are working for a gift, then it is no longer a gift! Heaven is a free gift from God for all of who have accepted Jesus Christ as Savior and Lord of their lives. It is free because Jesus Christ has already paid the price for it. Romans 6:23 reminds us that even though the "wages of sin is death," we can rest assured that we don't have to experience that death because "the free gift of God is eternal life in Christ Jesus our lord."

So, eternal life is not earned or deserved, but has been reserved for all of humanity. There's only one problem—sin. As a matter of fact, when it comes to humanity, we are all born with a sin nature. To sin means to fall short of the mark. The Message Bible shares an interesting explanation concerning how the first man, Adam, brought sin into the world in Romans 5:12-14.

> You know the story of how Adam landed us in the dilemma we're in—first sin, then death, and no one exempt from either sin or death. That sin disturbed relations with God in everything and everyone, but the extent of the disturbance was not clear until God spelled it out in detail to Moses. So death, this huge abyss separating us from God, dominated the landscape from Adam to Moses. Even those who didn't sin precisely as Adam did by disobeying a specific command of God still had to experience this termination of life, this separation from God. But Adam, who got us into this, also points ahead to the One who will get us out of it.

So, the reality is that we are all sinners. Romans 3:23 states, "for all have sinned and fall short of the glory of God." In addition to the fact that we are all sinners, we cannot save ourselves. The Apostle Paul confirms this in Ephesians 2:8-9, "For by grace you have been saved through faith. And this is not of your own doing; it is the gift of God, not a result of works, so that no one may boast." It's a gift plain and simple. No amount of arguing or striving will change that—so just accept it for what it is—an incredible gift.

Another wonderful thing about God is that he's merciful. He doesn't take great delight in punishing us. But God is also a just God, so he must punish sin. Romans 6:23 states, "For the wages of sin is death, but the free gift of God is eternal life in Christ Jesus our lord." That's why God sent his only son, Jesus Christ, to die on a cross for us. As a matter of fact, John 3:16 reveals a great truth, in that God loved his creation so much that "he gave his only son" to endure crucifixion and death in payment for the sins of the world.

This was due to the Old Testament requirement that sins must be atoned for—or payment for forgiveness—by the shedding of blood. The writer of Hebrews helps us see this when speaking about the Old Testament priestly functions in Hebrews 9:21-22, "And in the same way he sprinkled with the blood both the tent and all the vessels used in worship. Indeed, under the law almost everything is purified with blood, and without the shedding of blood there is no forgiveness of sins." Hebrews 10:3-4 proclaims a great truth, "But in these sacrifices there is a reminder of sins every year. For it is impossible for the blood of bulls and goats to take away sins." What a weight to carry! You could pay for your sins, but you could never be allowed to forget. God knew that humankind could not save themselves, so he made a way of forgiveness through the sacrifice of His only son. Because of His great sacrifice, we can find forgiveness and no longer have to be continually reminded of our sins. That's God-sized mercy! When we are in Christ, "all things become new" (2 Corinthians 5:17), because He paid the price for sins once and for all.

But who is this Christ? The one who was fully God and fully man. John 1:1 tells us, "In the beginning was the Word, and the Word was with God, and the Word was God." And later in John 1:14, "And the Word became flesh and dwelt among us, and we have seen his glory, glory as of the only Son from the Father, full of grace and truth." Jesus Christ was God's only son who paid for our sins and purchased a place in heaven for us, which he offers as a gift.

Interestingly, gifts are usually planned for long before they are given. So, let's take a trip back in time to the beginning. God knew that His creation would need His guidance, provision, and protection. Scriptures often refer to God's creation as sheep—a needy animal. Ezekiel 34:31 depicts God talking about his chosen nation of Israel, but the verse applies to all of God's creation, "And you are my sheep, human sheep of my pasture, and I am your God, declares the Lord God." And like sheep, we wanted to go wherever we wanted. The Old Testament prophet Isaiah shares with us in Isaiah 53:6, "All we like sheep have gone astray; we have turned—every one—to his own way; and the Lord has laid on him the iniquity of us all." The Apostle Paul sheds some light on the meaning of this when he states in Romans 5:8, "But God shows his love for us in that while we were still sinners, Christ died for us." Even though we all have a tendency to go our own way as Isaiah shares, Christ still died to make provision for the restoration of a right relationship with God. That's why faith is so important.

Hebrews 11:1 tells us, "Now faith is the substance of things hoped for, the evidence of things not seen." This means that faith is not merely your intellectual assent nor a temporal kind of faith. It is a continual faith that places complete trust in God. Remember what Paul said in Ephesians 2:8 (KJV), "For by grace are you saved *through faith*; and that not of yourselves: it is the gift of God: Not of works, lest any man should boast." [Emphasis added]

This faith that the Apostle Paul talks about is trusting in Jesus Christ alone for our salvation, or gift from God. Romans 10:9 clearly assures us of a divine truth, "If you confess with your mouth that Jesus is Lord and believe in your heart that God raised him from the dead, you will be saved." Romans 10:13 further clarifies this truth for us, "For, everyone who calls on the name of the Lord will be saved." It is a simple acknowledgement that doesn't take a lot of time. I love what Billy Graham stated in his 1957 crusade when talking about how long it takes for Christ to change your heart. He snapped his fingers and said, "That long." It's immediate, but is based on a person's true faith and belief in Christ as their personal Lord and Savior.

The writer of Hebrews 12:2 explains why every person needs to ask Jesus Christ to be the Lord of his or her life and to forgive them of their sins. "Looking unto Jesus the author and finisher of our faith; who for the joy that was set before him endured the cross, despising the shame, and is set down at the right hand of the throne of God." You see, we all put Jesus Christ on the cross. He alone bore the pain and suffering of the crucifixion and the beatings preceding it for the sins of the whole world.

We live in a fallen world. So even the very best person in a fallen world still falls short of a perfect God. I have heard some people say, "Well, I just need to get things cleaned up a little in my life and then I'll get back in church." My response to that is, "How does a fallen person, in a fallen world, get cleaned up enough to earn the right to be in the presence of a Holy, sinless, God who created the universe?" That doesn't make sense. It just cannot happen that way.

When seeking whether the person you are talking to is ready to make a commitment by asking for God's forgiveness of their sins and committing their lives to Christ, some questions might be in order. You might want to ask, "Does this make sense to you?" Or, "Is there any reason you wouldn't want to invite Christ into your heart and enjoy his forgiveness in your life?" You might ask, "Would you like to receive this free gift of eternal life that the Bible talks about?

Whatever the response, be prepared to clarify further and ensure that the person understands that he or she is asking Jesus Christ to forgive him or her of their sins and invite Him to have Lordship and leadership of his or her life. As I've shared earlier, there are many differing prayers you can pray, but sincerity is the most important aspect of this prayer of invitation and commitment. Another example is:

Dear Jesus, here I am. I'm not perfect. I'm a sinner and I need a savior. Would you forgive me of my sins, and be the lord of my life? Would you come into my heart right now, and help me live for you all the days of my life? In Jesus name, amen.

One of the most important keys to share if you have had the privilege of praying this prayer with someone, is to help the new believer hold on to this new-found faith. A great Scripture to verify their forgiveness and encourage a new believer's faith is found in 2 Corinthians 5:17, "Therefore, if anyone is in Christ, he is a new creation. The old has passed away; behold, the new has come."

Follow-up

The one thing you never want to do after introducing people to Christ, is fail to follow-up with them if at all possible. You need to get contact information or at the very least give them your contact information and invite them to call you in the days ahead.

Some immediate follow-up[118] information might include: giving them a Bible if they do not have one and sharing a "first steps" brochure or booklet that might help a new believer have some regular Bible reading time every day.

Another area of follow-up is prayer. Keep this person on your prayer list and also add them to your church's prayer list so that the Holy Spirit will continue to help protect and guide this new believer in the direction that would be most helpful for them.

---

118 Kennedy, 135.

Invite this new believer to your church if possible and sit with them if they are able to come. Having a friend in an unfamiliar environment is worth its weight in gold. Share what has happened with your church leadership and work with them to help this new believer engage in church activities, fellowship, and the sharing of their testimony.

A final word for you...

Please don't feel like you have to follow every step that I've talked about here! It's okay to skip around and share what is relevant or how you feel the Holy Spirit is leading you to share. Secondly, as I've shared before, don't try to be somebody else—you are who you are, and authenticity goes a long way to put others at ease. Most importantly, don't worry about fruit—that's God's business. He's the only real soulwinner anyway.

YOUR ASSIGNMENT:
Reflection, Sharing, And Application

1. Memorize the seven Scriptures that have been mentioned in this chapter. Take one each week and put it in visible places where you live and work. At the very least, you should have these Scriptures memorized in seven weeks. People at work may even ask you what you are doing and that would be a great opportunity to share that you just want to share about the awesome things God has done in your life with others. That's why you are trying to memorize some important Scripture verses. Then you could ask, "Do you read the Bible much?" and let God do the rest.

2. Write out in your own words what "Being Saved" means to you. This will help you if someone you are witnessing to asks that challenging question.

3. Think through how you might pray the prayer of salvation when you ask someone, "Is there anything keeping you from asking Jesus Christ into your heart?"

4. Now that you are equipped with your testimony and some great Scriptures, ask God for opportunities to share the hope that is within you. Write down how you feel the Holy Spirit is leading you.

5. Whatever experience you have, tell someone in your circle of friends or your small group what happened and ask them what they might have done differently.

6. Whatever experience you have in sharing your faith, take a moment to thank God for even giving you that opportunity to scatter some Gospel seed. You never know who might be listening either, so don't beat yourself up if things did not go as planned. God's in charge and He gets all the glory anyway.

7. Remember, God has commanded every believer to do this. The fact that you even made the effort is a huge accomplishment. Congratulations!

CHAPTER 9

RELAY...BY LIVING LIKE AN AMBASSADOR

As Christians, we must all understand the importance of living the life that we exhort others to live. In short, we must be ambassadors for Jesus Christ and allow the light of Christ to shine through our lives as spiritual lighthouses in a world full of dark places. Fortunately:

> 'Being an ambassador for Christ really means being who we are already at our best or who we would love to be!' When enough of our people discover that, they will realize that they may be the best-prepared generation in centuries to fulfill the Great Commission. If enough of us discover this, our churches will become unstoppable movements.[119]

When we live our lives in a Christlike manner, others will notice and permit us opportunities to speak into their lives. God is working in our lives (Philippians 2:13) and Paul encourages us in our walk, "that you may be blameless and innocent, children of God without

---

119 George G. Hunter III, *The Apostolic Congregation*, 83.

blemish in the midst of a crooked and twisted generation, among whom you shine as lights in the world" (Philippians 2:15). Even when people don't tell you, they are prone to respect a person who lives what they teach.

In Matthew chapter five, Jesus shares what are called "The Beatitudes" wherein he begins by saying, "Blessed are the poor in spirit..." and proceeds to give a litany of other attributes that are blessed. Immediately following these verses, Jesus reveals how his followers are salt and light to a world that has a broken relationship with God and is lost without Him. In verses thirteen through sixteen Jesus says:

[13] *You are the salt of the earth, but if salt has lost its taste, how shall its saltiness be restored? It is no longer good for anything except to be thrown out and trampled under people's feet.*

[14] *You are the light of the world. A city set on a hill cannot be hidden.* [15] *Nor do people light a lamp and put it under a basket, but on a stand, and it gives light to all in the house.* [16] *In the same way, let your light shine before others, so that they may see your good works and give glory to your Father who is in heaven.*

Sometimes, you may hear the word "lost" to depict someone who does not know Christ. Being "lost" does not mean that a person cannot function, but that they are trying to follow a less than perfect path for their life—similar to a lost sheep. Lost sheep need someone to lead and guide them along the right paths to safety, security, and sustenance. As followers of Jesus Christ, each one of us has been called to be spiritual salt and light to those who do not know Jesus Christ.

I know that sometimes it is difficult to navigate life's landscapes. It would be great if I had this spiritual lighthouse that would always give me direction, always show me the right way, always reveal the obstacles and dangers that are in front of me. But I don't have a lighthouse and neither do you. What Christians do have is far better, "Again, Jesus spoke to them, saying, 'I am the light of the world. Whoever follows me will not walk in darkness, but will have the light of life" (John 8:12). God not only illuminates our way, but He uses people to shine that light for others and act as ambassadors for Him—urging the unbeliever to follow Him. "No one ever came to Christ without some sort of proclamation and persuasion. We are called to present the Good News for acceptance. God calls people through people, for 'we are ambassadors for Christ, as though God were making an appeal through us; we beg you on behalf of Christ, be reconciled to God' (2 Corinthians 5:20). This is our role. May we be obedient."[120]

Speaking of lighthouses, I remember a mission trip to South Africa that our family experienced years ago. While in country, we had the opportunity see Cape Point, which is the southernmost point of Africa. We also went to the Cape of Good Hope, which is the southwest most southern part of Africa. Thankfully, they are only separated by about five minutes of roadway! They are not far apart, but they both have their own individual lookout points. Upon the high cliff setting at Cape Point, there is a lighthouse. It is there because the Indian and Atlantic oceans meet at the southern point of Africa, and ships need the assistance of a lighthouse in those often-rough seas along the rocky coastline there.

Now, the lighthouse is an interesting structure because it provides a couple of important things. It helps sailors avoid danger; but it also provides comfort. It helps to avoid danger by warning others about dangerous places, which gives the opportunity to make a decision or a choice to change course. Caroline Schoeder stated,

---

120 Gary L. McIntosh, *Growing God's Church: How People Are Actually Coming To Faith Today* (Grand Rapids, MI: Baker Books, 2016), 63.

"Some people change their ways when they see the light; others when they feel the heat."[121] I think she was talking about me! I don't know about you, but sometimes I just need the Lord to hit me upside the head in order to get my attention. For some reason, usually when I'm extremely busy, I seem to miss those gentle nudges from the Holy Spirit. I think if I just had more flashing lighthouses, sirens, or God speaking in a loud, thunderous voice, I would get the hint much easier. Do you ever feel like that?

Thankfully, the Lord loves to help us change course when needed and he helps us in the most unexpected ways! He will illuminate those things that are not good for us and almost shout: "Hey! If you go down that direction, you're going to be in really big trouble!"

Additionally, a lighthouse provides comfort. We can associate a lighthouse with comfort because—as many of you realize—it is wonderful to know where you are and where you are going! When serving in the military, they used to drop our group in the middle of nowhere, give us a compass, and say, "Here's a map so find your way home." That was a true test of your faith in the equipment and ability to use it. It is good to know where you are and how to find your way around the landscape where you are located. That's why a lighthouse is so nice.

My musings about a lighthouse started me thinking about spiritual lighthouses and the Christian's role as an ambassador for Christ. I began to ponder how we can be the kind of spiritual lighthouses that God desires in life. In our communities, our workplace, or wherever we find ourselves. As followers of Christ, God has called us to live a lighthouse kind of life. A life that helps provide direction and comfort to others who are searching for a

---

121 See this and other people changing quotes at http://www.wiseoldsayings.com/people-changing-quotes/

better way. And if you are going to live a lighthouse kind of life, you must understand two very important keys.

A VISIBLE LIFE

The Right Element

The first key you must understand is that a lighthouse kind of life is a visible life. And if you are going to be visible, you must have the right element. Thomas Edison discovered that reality while conducting all his experiments leading up to the creation of the lightbulb. Without the right element, a lighthouse is merely another historic landmark. In the community where you live, there may be many landmarks—statues, monuments, and other wonderful emblems that remind us of our history—good and bad. But God wants you and me to be living, breathing, spiritual lighthouses for Him. He is a living God not a dead one—a God who hears and answers our prayers when we call out to Him.

In Matthew 5:13, Jesus compares us to salt—sodium chloride—common table salt. Initially, I'm thinking that's not much of a compliment. I haven't heard anyone tell me lately, "Wow, you're looking salty tonight!" and feel as though I just received a huge compliment. As a matter of fact, calling someone salty usually means that they are a pretty tough character. But, in biblical times it was a different story altogether. So, what do we use salt for today? To add flavor to our food. You don't add salt to your food just because you enjoy looking at the white sprinkles and thinking, "Wow! Now that is a decorative spice!" If that's so, then let it snow on my meat and potatoes! But actually, salt does something to our food—it adds flavor. It makes a difference! I know you're starting to get the spiritual picture, aren't you?

In ancient times, salt was known for its preservative[122] qualities among numerous other characteristics—both good and bad. Preservation of food was one of its better uses. Without salt, there was no way to preserve meat for any lengthy period of time. Normally, people would have to seek out food products on a daily basis since there was no way to keep them from spoiling. The history books tell us that at one point there were caravans as large as forty thousand camels long[123] bearing salt crossing the Sahara Desert—it was valuable! I don't know about you, but I have a hard time getting my mind around a caravan that large.

I experienced the value of salt myself as a young boy growing up on the farm. We would butcher our own hogs in winter time to help feed our family of ten. When it came time to hang up the ham and bacon, a "salt cure" mixture of salt and other spices would be applied to help keep the meat from spoiling while it "cured" in the smoke house for months. As a matter of fact, some sources say that salt was known as the cornerstone of modern civilization due to the multitude of uses and the importance of salt in our daily diets. There can be no doubt that salt has had an important part to play in history.

The Latin word for salt is *salis,* which is the basis for the Latin word, *salarium,* meaning a payment in salt. Oftentimes, government workers would receive payments in salt.[124] This is also where we get one of our most favorite words—salary! Now, how would you like someone backing up a dump truck in your driveway? Then saying, "Hey, I just wanted to make a down payment on the debt I owe!"

---

122 Leland Ryken et al., eds., *Dictionary of Biblical Imagery* (Downers Grove, IL: InterVarsity, 1998), s.v. "Salt."

123 For more information about these read "Salt Caravans," at https://quatr.us/food-2/salt-caravans.htm

124 For more reading on salt go to https://www.seasalt.com/history-of-salt

Then proceed to unload that salt on your driveway. Somehow, I just don't think you're going to be as excited about that as opposed to someone dumping a load of gold on your driveway. I like salt, but I'd rather have the gold!

We appreciate salt when we need to clear the sidewalks on a snowy day, keep the roadways from freezing over, or add a little flavor to our food, but that's about as far as our appreciation goes today. However, in ancient times salt was an extremely valuable commodity. Salt also had great anti-bacterial uses and thus, it's preservative qualities.

An interesting characteristic of sodium—a part of sodium chloride or regular table salt—is that is it never found by itself in the natural. It is always found with another element. The Holy Spirit seemed to nudge me one day about an intriguing parallel between the similarities of sodium and our relationship with God. You see, God never intended us to walk this journey called life alone. God always wanted to be with us throughout our journey. As a matter of fact, in John 1:4 we're told, "In him was life, and the life was the light of men." In Christ, there is illumination as we travel along life's journey. Jesus Christ wants to be your eternal "B.F.F."—your eternal Best Friend Forever. I'm sure there are many people who might like to be your B.F.F. until you die, but Jesus is that eternal best friend that is closer—even closer than a brother (Proverbs 18:24). We can all use a friend like that.

But in order for people to have that living relationship with Jesus Christ, we must have a right relationship with Him. We must allow Jesus Christ to have an "All Access" pass to every area of our lives. Many of us will let God into our lives to some extent, but we usually label some areas as "off limits." If we're not going to let God have full access, how can we get upset when we feel that He has betrayed us, or misled us, or we lost communication somehow? Also, how are we going to tell others about a Christ that we're afraid to let into every area of our lives? We must come to the place where we can trust God to do what is best for us every single time, only then can we honestly share the goodness of God without reservation. We may not like, understand, or enjoy some of life's encounters, but faith assures us that God will do what's best.

I like to talk to people about what happens when God comes to their house. It's similar to a guest who comes to your home. We like to clean up the front part of the house, but we have these certain rooms that are off limits. I don't know about you, but Nancy and I have never asked someone visiting our house to look in the utility closet and inspect it for us. Or how about the master bedroom, garage, or all the kids' rooms—nope—they're all off limits. I have been in homes where you would swear there are only two rooms accessible—the living room and the dining room, and "No, we don't need any help in the kitchen!" We just have certain places in our homes where we have cleaned up and allowed other people access when they come to visit.

Similarly, we often do the very same thing in the spiritual arena. We say, "Hey God. I don't mind you coming in and helping me on the job and other important things. But you know all these other little fears that I have? And these other challenges that I have? And these issues that trip me up on occasion? You can just leave those alone because I'm dealing with them myself." In essence we're telling God, "I'm not really ready for you to come in and help me." But as an ambassador, we cannot have that kind of attitude about the One we represent.

You see, God wants the whole house—your whole spiritual house. He wants all of us. He wants to have that intimate relationship with you. As a matter of fact, in John 15:5, Jesus says: "I am the vine, you are the branches, if a man remains in me and I in him, he will bear much fruit, but apart from me you can do nothing." He wants to have this healthy relationship with us, and when we have that, we can do all kinds of unimaginable things for the Kingdom of God—like have faith conversations. But Jesus is saying, without me you can do nothing. Now, He's not saying that you cannot function if you do not have a right relationship with Him. Sure, you can function and live life without Him, but you cannot do anything of eternal consequence with God unless you are a part of the body—or family—of Christ.

As a matter of fact, Jesus continues in John 15:6, "If anyone does not remain in me, he is like a branch that is thrown away and withers. Such branches are picked up, thrown into the fire and burned." Jesus is telling you and me that bad salt and dead branches are treated the same way. They are discarded. They are thrown away. And if you and I are not maintaining a right relationship with Jesus Christ, we are going to spiritually die. We are going to wither. We will be cast aside and on the Day of Judgment we will be discarded. You cannot be an ambassador if you have no relationship to, or authority from, the one you represent. But Jesus is that anti-bacterial—if you will—in our lives. He is helping you and me maintain our spiritual saltiness. I don't know about you, but I want more of Christ in my life today than I had yesterday! I want to be so filled with God's Holy Spirit that His overflowing presence in my life just spills out on someone. I hope you do, too! I want people to ask me, "Man, what's wrong with you?" Then I can say, "Oh my goodness, I went to church today! You should come with me next Sunday!"

You see, if good salt touches anything, it will effect change. Just like a light in a lighthouse, but you have to have the right element. That's why you and I need the element of Jesus Christ in our lives. With Christ in our lives, we have the authority and relationship to act in a powerful way that's pleasing to our heavenly Father and blameless in this world.

The Right Location

Not only do we need to have the right element if we plan on having a visible life, but we also need to have the right location. I have often noticed that lighthouses are scarce when you travel inland from the coast line anywhere in the world. In Dallas, Texas; Springfield, Missouri; Des Moines, Iowa; Frankfort, Germany; Barcelona, Spain; Nairobi, Kenya; or any other number of places far from the coast, you rarely see a lighthouse unless it is purely for decoration. You just don't see real lighthouses unless you are on the coastline or the Great Lakes in the United States. They are in strategic places! Jesus even reminds us in Matthew 15:14, "You are the light of the world. A city set on a hill cannot be hidden." What does that tell us today? That tells us that a Christian cannot hide—and you shouldn't want to hide—because God has placed you in a strategic place for His light to shine through you.

I remember when my daughter, Hannah, was around five years old, we would play a game of hide and seek. I would come home from the office, and when I came through the door, I knew she was hiding. So, my goal was to find her as soon as I walked through the door, because I knew she wanted to be found. You might ask, "Well, Marshall, how did you know she wanted you to find her?" That's a great question! There were these little indicators that told me Hannah wanted to be found. Like, the leg that is sticking out from behind the chair. Or, the eyes peeking out from behind a door that isn't quite open all the way. Or, the giggling that would come from behind the shower curtain. These little indicators confirmed to me that Hannah wanted to be found by her daddy.

Today, there are a lot of people in the world who want to be found. As a matter of fact, "Christianity teaches that lost people cannot, by themselves, find the life that they deeply want and were meant for. They search for life, but in all the wrong places. Lost people need to be found; if they are to be found, they are more likely to be found on their turf than in churches!"[125] We can look in the newspaper to see how depression and other challenges seem to be increasing without any age limits. From elementary schools to retirement homes, people are looking for answers right in our own communities. We often follow the secular reasoning of what it takes to find happiness, with meager lasting results—if any. I tried that for almost fifteen years and it just did not work, because God has a special place in every person's life that is reserved just for Him.

Today, I want to encourage you. God has put you in a strategic place because you are a very special person to Him. He has put every single one of us in strategic places to share the light of Jesus Christ. And granted, where you are might be hard. It might be tough. It might be very difficult. It might be dark. It might be really challenging. But isn't that where a lighthouse is supposed to be? Now, I'm not advocating people being in abusive relationships or anything like that. You need to find help to deliver you from that kind of treatment. But just because a place is hard does not mean that it's not God's place for you. It's right where a spiritual lighthouse and Christ's ambassador need to be in order to help bring about change!

When the Lord moved us from Springfield, Missouri to Tyler, Texas it felt as though the gates of hell just flung open. It seemed like the Devil was saying, "Hey, Marshall's free, let's get him!" We faced one challenge after another, after another. I was like, "God? Do you know what you're doing? Did I make a wrong decision? Did I take a wrong turn?" No. God needed some prayer warriors right where we were living. God wanted to take me into a closer relationship with Him and teach me some important spiritual lessons, because He wanted me to be a light to the community where I lived.

---

125 George G. Hunter III, *Go: The Church's Main Purpose* (Nashville, TN: Abingdon, 2017), 83.

Sadly, many Christians embrace the thought, "Well, I can't really do much. I mean who am I? I am just one person." Thoughts like that remind me of a situation that happened many years ago wherein my similar attitude was totally changed. One of the fun activities we used to do when beginning our ministry was to visit places that would interest our children. Most of those places were free. I love free! And one of the things we loved to do involved visiting natural caves located in state parks.

Now, when you go into a cave, you wander through the tunnels and caverns, looking at all the formations that the guide points out. Eventually, they take you to the last cavern or room in the cave, and what do they do when you get to that last room? Yep—they turn the lights out and tell you, "Well, we just want you to see what the first explorers saw when they came here." After you have seen as many caves as we had, you get to the point of having the same expectation: "Okay, the lights go out and I can't see my hand in front of my face. Thank you very much. Lights on. Get the T-shirt. Next cave." You can tell, I wasn't quite as moved by the experiences as I should have been!

But in one particular cave, we found ourselves in a huge cavern at the end of the tour. And sure enough, after the lights went out, the guide said, "Now, I want you to see what the first explorers saw when they came into this cave." But differently than the other tours we had experienced, he merely struck a match and lifted it up. When he lifted that match, we could see the far side of that cavern! You might say, well that's not so surprising. But the cavern we stood in was as big as a football stadium. It was huge! I couldn't believe that a single match could illuminate an immense cavern to the point that I could see the far wall on the opposite side.

When I thought about that experience, I was reminded of how darkness is merely the absence of light. God wants you and I to be the lighthouses that He has called us to be right where we live. God's going to do what is needful. He's going to work through you if you let Him. But you and I have to be faithful to look for those divine appointments and share the hope that is within us when God gives us that gentle nudge. Don't ever think that you cannot do anything. God has so much more that He wants you and I to do—we just don't know about it yet!

Sharing the hope that is within us is one of those things we can do that is a bit easier than most of us honestly believe. John 1:6-7 says, "There was a man sent from God, whose name was John. He came as a witness, to bear witness about the light, that all might believe through him." Jesus is talking about John the Baptist. The King James translation states that he came to "bear witness of the light." In the original Greek language of the New Testament, some variants of this word for bear witness or testify, can convey the meaning "to speak well of."[126]

As Christians, how many of us have nothing good to say about what God has done in our lives? Nobody! Every single one of us should be able to say something good about our lives since we met Jesus Christ. God is looking for you and me to take up for, or defend, Him—to speak well of Him! I came from a family of eight children. My brothers and sisters could really give me a hard time and push me around when we were growing up. But if anyone else gave any of us a hard time—you got the whole Windsor clan! Ironically, there are times when I visit the old hometown, and someone asks, "You're a Windsor, aren't you?" At that point I have a sudden fear that it may not be a pleasant recollection. None of us were perfect, so I quit trying to act like it—but what a great opportunity to slip in a good word for the Lord! So, I can respond, "Yes sir, we probably tested a lot of folks in our early years, but the good Lord and I are

---

126 "Martureo." In *Shorter Lexicon of the Greek New Testament*, 2 ed. Rev. (Chicago, IL: University of Chicago Press, 1983), 122.

on better speaking terms now. How about yourself?" Then let the Holy Spirit steer the conversation!

I grew up in a smaller community that had the typical challenges of all smaller communities. It almost seemed like everyone else knew your business; and whatever they did not know they just made up. Over the years I've noticed most folks tend to agree that smaller communities have some peculiar dynamics—often just like a really large family. But the reality is that there are challenges wherever we live. Our family seemed to thrive in the local community, but we always took up for each other. In like manner, God is looking for folks who will take up for Him—so be ready to say something good about Him!

God is the author of salvation and is the one who will bring the unbeliever to a point of decision. He is the one who changes a person's life. Someone's salvation decision is not necessarily dependent upon how good you can present the Gospel. As John 1:6-7 reveals, God is almost saying, "Why don't you just take up for me? Why don't you just tell them what God's done in your life?" We can all say, "He's changed me. He's lifted me up." Greg Koukl states it concisely: "As ambassadors, we measure our legitimacy by faithfulness and obedience to Christ, who alone will bring the increase. The most important gauge of our success will not be our numbers or even our impact, but our fidelity to our Savior."[127]

You see, our lives provide opportunities for other people to change theirs. Can I say that one more time? Our lives provide opportunities for other people to change theirs. God wants to use you. He wants you to be that spiritual lighthouse in your workplace and in your community that helps other people see His goodness. God longs for you to be a lighthouse that is visible. And if you plan on being visible, you must have the right element and you must be

---

127 Gregory Koukl, *Tactics*, 198.

in the right location. You must be where God wants you to be—right in the center of His will.

A VALUABLE LIFE

It Belongs To God

Not only is a lighthouse kind of a life a visible life; it's a valuable life. As an ambassador of Christ, we are subject to his authority and have a special relationship to God that has been purchased by Jesus Christ. As a matter of fact, Paul takes this a step further in 1 Corinthians 6:19-20. "Or do you not know that your body is the temple of the Holy Spirit within you, whom you have from God? You are not your own, for you were bought with a price. So, glorify God in your body." Each one of God's children is valuable to Him—whether you feel like it or not. Just like a physical lighthouse costs a lot of money to build, a great price was paid in order that we could have a right relationship with God. Jesus Christ was beaten beyond recognition and nailed to a cross to pay the cost of the sin nature with which we all wrestle. He paid a great price to be the light of men (John 1:4).

The Apostle Paul told the Corinthians—and us today—in 2 Corinthians 5:21, "For he hath made him to be sin for us [talking of Jesus Christ], who knew no sin; that we might be made the righteousness of God in him." You and I did not have to do anything to earn this priceless gift. Our only effort was to acknowledge our fallen state, ask forgiveness, and receive this free gift from God, becoming the righteousness of God in Him. When we let Jesus Christ become lord and leader of our lives, we have just become the righteousness of God because we take on the righteousness of Christ. All of this merely because we are in a right relationship with Jesus Christ by accepting Him as our lord and savior.

Salvation had an expensive price tag for God, but it is expensive for us, too. Because, when we allow Jesus Christ an opportunity to rule and reign in our lives, He calls us to walk away from some things in order to be the kind of lighthouse He desires. Personally, I walked away from smoking and that hasn't seemed to hurt me too much. I walked away from chewing tobacco and using snuff. I walked away from drinking anything with alcohol and started treating ladies with respect. I even had to give up some of my friends. I did not intentionally give them up, they just left. They walked away because they did not like the change in me.

Then there were the job opportunities that did not materialize because of where I stood as a Christian. When that happens, I truly believe God always has something better, because as Christians, we have someone who is on our side—an advocate. There is an intercessor, named Jesus Christ, who is interceding for everyone who has accepted Him. It doesn't matter where we are in life or the troubles that we go through, there is somebody who is praying for us! Jesus is on our side. So, when job opportunities vanish, look up because God's got something great—or someone—headed your way. So, keep shining your light!

Jesus confirms how expensive it is in Luke 9:23, "And he said to them all, 'If anyone would come after me, let him deny himself and take up his cross daily and follow me.'" The Message translation shares an interesting perspective:

Anyone who intends to come with me has to let me lead. You're not in the driver's seat—I am. Don't run from suffering; embrace it. Follow me and I'll show you how.

God is so gracious that He will show us how to follow Him if we will embrace Him and His word. Obviously, there is a cost to discipleship—or a commitment that's needed to follow Christ. That doesn't come overnight, but through a process. Michael Green aptly states concerning a person's cost of following Christ: "There is something to **admit**—that he is not in living touch with God and needs to get right with him. There is something to **believe**—that God in Christ has done everything needed for our restoration. There is something to **consider**—the cost of discipleship. There is something to **do**—to reach out in faith, and personally appropriate the proffered gift."[128] Dietrich Bonhoeffer offers a plainer reality about the cost of discipleship: "When Christ calls a man, He bids him come and die."[129] He meant that we must all die to our selfishness and pursue the Christ of Calvary—costly indeed!

Aren't you glad Jesus didn't try to deceive us about the cost of following Him? He candidly told us that if they persecuted Him, then we could expect the same. But He said He would be with us—and the people you interact with every day need to hear that. "God delights in using ordinary Christians who come to the end of themselves and choose to trust in His extraordinary provision."[130] When we deny ourselves and trust Christ, we'll see the miraculous take place: from changed lives to divine provision. The people in your community, where you live, work, shop, go to school, ride the subway or metro, do your banking, get your hair cut or permed—they all need to know God's on their side.

The Scriptures exhort us to deny ourselves and our self-regard if we want to see spiritual fruit, which is usually necessary if we are going to shine the light of Christ instead of our own—much dimmer—light. Honestly, that doesn't come naturally for most of

---

128 Michael Green, *Sharing Your Faith With Family And Friends* (Grand Rapids, MI: Baker, 2005), 81.

129 Dietrich Bonhoeffer, *The Cost of Discipleship,* rev. ed. (New York: Macmillan, 1963), 99.

130 David Platt, *Radical: Taking Back Your Faith From The American Dream* (Colorado Springs, CO: Multnomah, 2010), 56.

us. It takes the indwelling Holy Spirit of God, drawing us closer to our heavenly Father, that compels us to sacrifice. We all enjoy acceptance from others. I don't want my friends making fun of me. However, I've come to the place where my relationship with God is more important than anything else. When that relationship is healthy everything else works out fine.

In Matthew 5:15, Jesus said: "nor do people light a lamp and put it under a basket, but on a stand, and it gives light to all in the house." If we hide in the church or in our homes no one will see the light. God doesn't want us to hide the light of Christ in our lives, he wants us to go out into our communities and be a blessing to others. He wants us to share that light of Christ within us and let it shine wherever we find ourselves.

Don't you show off what you are proud of? What you're excited about? Those things and people that mean a lot to you? I remember my first car growing up. It was a used, black 1964 Ford, Galaxy 500. We called that car the Black Beauty. I would drive seven miles to town because I wanted to cruise Main Street and show off my car, but then it would overheat on the way back home. That never bothered me because that was my car! That was my baby!

My dad originally purchased that car for my sisters, who had requested an old car with some dents. They confessed that if they put more dents in it no one would care. Now, driving wasn't necessarily as important to them as it was to me. One of my sisters ended up driving that car right into a ditch, which bent a steering tie rod (a 1-inch metal rod) and put a hole in the radiator. After which, my sister declared that she wasn't driving again. Being the kind person I was [sarcasm added], I asked: "Can I have it?" Granted I was only fifteen at the time, but I really wanted a car and I was willing to fix that one and wait until I turned sixteen to drive it (on the official roads). To my surprise, they said they didn't care!

I said great! So, I soldered the hole in the radiator and took a ten-pound sledge hammer to the tie rod and straightened it out the best I could. No one had informed me that tie rods could not be straightened! Then, I did the best I could to align the front end and called it good. I drove that car around the farm for six months until I turned sixteen. It was my car. I would drive that car into town and cruise Main Street because I wanted everyone to know I had a car! Ironically, it was also the car I used to get my driver's license—on the third attempt.

I truly believe God is asking you and me a question: "Haven't I done something that's noteworthy, which you can brag about to others?" God longs to show Himself strong on our behalf (2 Chronicles 16:9) and He doesn't ask us to do something that's impossible. He is even there to help us! Matthew 19:26 tells us that "with God all things are possible." There is nothing too hard for God. From divine healing, to miraculous provision, to creating divine opportunities where we can say something good about him, to giving us the words to say, our heavenly Father is working on behalf of His children. That's why an ambassador for Christ is a lighthouse kind of life—which just so happens to be a valuable life—it belongs to God.

It's An Effective Life

A lighthouse kind of life and an ambassador for Christ is also valuable because it's effective. You see, there is life-changing power in a relationship with Jesus Christ. You are a great ambassador because you have experienced forgiveness! I know that God changed me and how that felt. If you have never had that life-changing experience with Christ, you can have it right now. Asking Jesus Christ to forgive you of your sins and letting him become the Lord of your life is the way to instantaneously have that lighthouse kind of life. And the reality is that this is a daily decision for every Christian who desires to have an effective life for the Kingdom of God, as we walk in our "new creation" bodies" (2 Corinthians 5:17).

Neither a lighthouse, nor an ambassador, is worth very much if it is not effective—if it doesn't work. A lighthouse must have a source of light for it to be effective. Similarly, Jesus Christ has to be the ultimate source of light for us as Christ's ambassadors, because He is the one who attracts other people. It is not our good looks or stunning personalities that draw people to Christ. The Holy Spirit alone draws people to Christ. Colossians 4:6 states: "Let your speech always be gracious, seasoned with salt, so that you may know how you ought to answer each person." You see, our answers ought to make other people thirsty for more of Christ. It's unnatural for anyone eating something salty to do so without anything to drink. That's why many drinking establishments often have lots of salty snacks. They know it makes customers thirsty!

Likewise, our conversations ought to cause people to thirst more after the Holy Spirit who resides within every true Christian. People we know might even ask us, "What's wrong with you?" or "What's going on in your life?" or "You just had someone pass away. How can you have so much peace?" or "Man, we all just lost our jobs. What's your problem? Aren't you stressed out about that?" Amazingly, you can answer, "No, because I serve the Prince of Peace."

I read once that spirit-filled believers shine forth and illuminate things as they really are. But why should we do that? Our passage of Scripture, and more specifically, Matthew 5:16, helps us see that other people are watching our actions and will see our "good" works. That word in the Greek is *kala*, which literally means good, better, proper, fitting, and right. The King James translation talks about the "better works." Other translations say, "better deeds." This means that Christians should set the standard. We don't need to cheat, lie, or steal in our daily dealings with others. We don't need to laugh at those off-color jokes that are sometimes heard in the workplace. We need to work at being a good example for others. The reason we should perform those better deeds is so that others will see them and become thirsty for more of God. They need to see that living a Godly life is a blessed life—and a life that blesses others.

The reality is that we are just a conduit for the Lord. A conduit is something we might see in a factory building. It is the metal tubing that often has electrical wire inside running to receptacle boxes throughout the building. That conduit provides protection and direction for what travels inside of it. As Christians, we are merely the spiritual fruit bearing branch on the vine. Have you ever seen a fruit tree eat its own fruit? Of course not. The fruit is for somebody else. Somebody who is not plugged into the vine. Somebody who is outside, if you will. The fruit is for them—those who do not have a saving knowledge of the Lord Jesus Christ. And Christians have the pleasure, with the life-giving presence of God that flows through His children, to produce that fruit and let it go. Since we're a part of the vine, we'll be able to produce another piece of fruit...and another...and another. What a blessing!

You and I do not need to hoard the blessings of God and never share them with others. It's through sharing with others what God has given us, that God's fruit maintains its freshness in our lives. God's Spirit helps us live as effective ambassadors for Christ—spiritual lighthouses that pour out blessings in our communities. If you had a glass of water sitting on your kitchen counter for two weeks and you had the option of drinking that or getting some fresh water from the faucet, which would you choose? I bet you prefer fresh water! God wants you and me to give away that life-giving spiritual water. Giving away the revelation of the Gospel of Jesus Christ to others is God's commission to us—even if it is only by the visible witness of our actions.

So, be the blessing that God has called you to be—His ambassador and spiritual lighthouse that serves as a conduit for the Gospel of Jesus Christ—the hope of the world. Pray for God's guidance in reaching out with a kind word to those people around you who are in dangerous waters. People who are living in dark, difficult, places. They need the light that Christ has entrusted to you. They've been waiting, watching, and hoping for someone who might have the answer to their feelings of lostness. That's what an ambassador for Christ and a lighthouse kind of life looks like. I'm praying it looks a lot like you—and God's got you covered.

Think About It

In 1869, the Cape Hatteras Lighthouse was built in North Carolina. It was known as the barber pole of North Carolina due to an error in painting by the engineers, who were originally supposed to paint it with diamonds instead of stripes. But it had warned sailors for over one hundred years of the dangerous Diamond Shoals sandbars that extended approximately fourteen miles out to sea. The lighthouse was around 225 feet tall with 268 steps going to the top. It was equipped with a light that shone roughly twenty-plus miles out to sea. But in 1999, due to erosion, they moved the lighthouse inland approximately one mile. Subsequently, they turned the lighthouse into a visitors' center; and now, it is no longer the effective lighthouse that it had originally been planned for in that area.

It is interesting to note the dynamic that happens when we move from where God has placed us—when our relationship with God grows distant. We become less and less effective as the vessels—the lighthouses—or the ambassadors that God has called us to be for Him. Can I ask you right now if you are where God wants you to be in your relationship with Him? Have you strayed from where God has originally called you to be? Have you wandered in your relationship with Jesus Christ? Have you allowed other things to distract you? You and I can only be truly effective in our efforts to share the hope within us when our relationship with God is healthy.

Unfortunately, it's so easy to stray from where God truly longs for us to be with Him. I remember a particular Sunday morning service in a small, country church early in our ministry years ago. When I finished speaking, folks began visiting and migrating toward the doors. One middle-aged gentleman came up to me after the service. He did not appear to be an exceptionally educated man, and I eventually discovered he didn't even have a high school education. However, he said to me, "You know Marshall. The Lord showed me a long time ago, that if the Devil can't get you sinning, he'll get you busy." I thought, what a jewel of wisdom. So often, we allow the numerous distractions of life to come in, and we begin to stray.

Right now is a great time to just take a moment and ask the Lord, "Am I where you want me to be in You? Is my relationship right with You? Have I moved God? Would you help me get back to the place where You want me to be?" It's a wonderful privilege to share the hope of Christ that is within every Christian. But we must ensure our relationship with Christ is healthy, because only He can help us truly live a lighthouse kind of life.

YOUR ASSIGNMENT:
Reflection, Sharing, Application

1. Select one day when you will set aside an hour or two of your time away from distractions to read the Bible, pray, and listen to God's nudging on what evangelism might look like in your life. You can even plan this as a group activity and share the following week some of the insights that God revealed to you.

2. Jot down your thoughts on what times, methods, and resources you might incorporate into your daily devotional time of Bible reading and prayer. This will stir up some great ideas! Ask your Christian friends or people in your group what they find helpful.

3. Write down your ideas about, or discuss with others, what a Gospel seed might look like as you practice living a lighthouse kind of life in relational evangelism.

4. Practice listing, finding and quoting Scripture that is relevant to sharing the Gospel with someone. You can share in a group or with partners. There are differing opinions on which Scriptures to memorize, but start with John 3:16, Romans 3:23, Romans 6:23, Romans 10:9, or some of your personal favorites that you may already know by heart.

5. Write down in your prayer journal, share with your group, or make a mental note about the one thing you could do that would improve your evangelism skills this next year.

CHAPTER 10

NEVER QUIT

L.E.A.R.N. Evangelism means to:

NEVER QUIT – Never quit looking for ways to scatter seeds of faith and hope in Jesus Christ.

Word association is powerful. If I say the word *popcorn*, you may start thinking of hot, buttery kernels that you can't get enough of as you watch a movie. You can almost smell the aroma right now because it is a smell that you love, and the more someone talks about it the more you want some right now! You may also have visions of cooking up your own batch of popcorn at home, and you can almost hear the pan screeching across the burner as you shake the pan and try to keep the kernels moving to avoid burning them. You can hear the popping kernels as they strike the metal pan and see the steam as you lift the lid and add your own flavoring. Delightful thoughts fill our minds when we think of something as pleasant as popcorn. By the way, my sister is the only person I have ever known who caught a panful of popcorn on fire and melted the knobs on the stove—but that's another story. If you've ever burned popcorn or gotten a bad batch, you didn't quit eating popcorn, you just moved on to the next batch because you have tasted the good stuff!

However, when I mention the word evangelism, we could often associate that word with fear, pushy, bigoted, arrogant, insensitive, embarrassing, or a plethora of other adjectives that are not too flattering. "Christians in general are afraid to use the word *evangelism*, as it recalls memories of judgmental people, forced presentations, talking to strangers, and unwise practices of proselytizing persons against their will."[131] But what if we started associating evangelism with God's possible view of that word: obedient, fulfilling, deliverance, healing, sensitive, sacrificial, unselfish, purpose, hope, love, compassion, life saver, hero, friend, family, kindness, or timely? When you and I are obedient and prepared to share the incredible things that God has done in our lives, the opportunities become less about our fearfulness or inadequacies and more about the need to help someone find answers, freedom, hope, and all those other words I just mentioned.

That is why we must never quit praying for opportunities and studying to find answers to questions that people are asking today. If you have ever encountered a bad faith-sharing experience—just like burned popcorn—don't quit looking for other opportunities. Just keep reminding yourself how awesome it feels when someone crosses that line of faith and asks Jesus Christ to be the Lord of their lives. People without Christ need some Good News—and God is hoping you and I will answer His call to tell them.

Never Quit Working On Your Testimony

When I have my testimony in written form, I can think through different strategies on how I might be able to use parts of it if I only have sixty seconds, a couple of minutes, or an hour over

---

131 Gary L. McIntosh, *Growing God's Church*, 20.

coffee. That's a goal you need to work towards. Never quit praying for opportunities to practice your sharing abilities or working on your testimony to see how you might be able to include parts of it in your everyday conversations. Be ready to ask someone, "Hey, what's the most amazing thing that's ever happened to you?" Then after they share their story, you can share yours. Here's a look at part of my testimony.

My Testimony

I was born into a middle-class family at Baylor hospital in Dallas, Texas at 4:54 in the morning in the summer of 1961. I'm sure by 4:54 in the morning my mother was ready for me to just get out! I don't remember much about those early years, except that we moved to Fort Worth when I was about four years old. School started for me just like most other kids at the age of five. But when I reached my sixth birthday, I had my own Stingray bicycle with a banana seat that I would ride to school. It was my pride and joy. Riding to school on a bike probably doesn't happen a lot these days for a six-year-old, but it was pretty standard transportation for young, city kids back in the 1960s. The city was my world until I hit the ripe old age of eight. Dad decided there was too much crime and so we moved to the farm—literally!

I learned a lot on the farm and gained a good work ethic. I discovered that chickens have a pecking order, which was pretty obvious when you saw the chicken who had the most feathers missing. I learned that there was only so far you wanted to go in cleaning out manure in a horse stall. Believe me when I tell you, sometimes it got pretty deep in there! My first job earned a whopping twenty-five cents an hour. But even an eight-year-old has limits when it comes to work and pay. After the first day of cleaning horse stalls I asked Dad for a raise—and got it! The next day I started at fifty cents an hour—and earned every penny. I learned about hauling hay, milking cows, and making sure the livestock were fed before I got to eat. That was a pretty normal life on the farm, but pretty different from city dwelling for sure.

I didn't really know that much about God or Jesus at the time, but I attended church along with my parents and seven other siblings. The summer I turned ten years old was the summer my life changed. I went to the Windermere music camp with our church group, and during one of the evening services the Holy Spirit touched my life. I remember sitting up close to the front, and not remembering much about what the preacher was actually saying. But, when the invitation to get things right with God was given, I knew I had to go. I was crying and didn't know why when asked by a counselor, but he finally probed a little deeper and discovered that I needed to ask Jesus Christ into my heart. When the service ended, I distinctly remembered walking outside the chapel and feeling as though I was walking on air. It was an amazing experience that I haven't forgotten after all these years!

After camp, I went home and began to read my Bible with a new hunger to know God. Unfortunately, I started in the Old Testament with a determination to read the entire Bible through at the ripe old age of ten. I only made it to Leviticus, when all the "begats" caused me to put my Bible back down. This, coupled with the fact that our church didn't really have any youth to interact with, caused me to fall back into fellowship with my worldly friends. By the age of thirteen I only went to church because my parents made me.

The following years were spent being somewhat rebellious and having fun in the world. I was sent to a military high school to help discipline me in my schoolwork and attitude. I did become more regimented in my attitude with more "ma'ams" and "sirs" becoming prevalent in my speech. My grades went from I (incompletes) to A. I graduated second in my small high school class of approximately thirty-six and had learned a lot about worldly people and worldly things, which became my focus. After graduating from Texas A&M University, where I studied agriculture, I went into the United States Army as a Field Artillery officer. It was during my tour in Germany that the Lord finally got a hold of me once again.

The pressures of military leadership, and my numerous additional duties, led to heavy drinking. I was pretty mean and cold hearted about a lot of things except my troops and my job. I was accumulating a lot of material things and money, but I wasn't happy. During all this time, I kept my Bible on my nightstand beside my bed. I never read it but wanted people to know I "had religion." I did not know that Christianity was all about a relationship with my heavenly Father. I was frustrated and desperate after trying to find peace and fulfillment on my own. It was at this point in my life that I finally picked up the Bible on my nightstand—one that my dad had given to me before I left for military service.

I knew it was time to give God one more chance, so I began reading my Bible every night before I went to bed. I thought things would automatically get better, but they didn't. About two weeks later, as I prayed, I made a decision to ask God to show me that He was real one more time. If I did not get any answers, I was going to put the Bible away once more. I just felt like I was at a crossroads and needed something that was missing in my life. Thankfully, God doesn't lead us to a point of decision to see us fail, but He is right there to help us make the right choice if we so desire.

As I prayed that night, I could sense a presence in the room that I had never felt before and I knew it could only be the Holy Spirit of God. My night lamp suddenly went dim, then bright, then dim, then bright once again. It had never done that in the two and a half years that I had been in Germany and it never did it again after that night. I truly believed that the Lord had answered my prayer and I sensed more than heard a still small voice saying, "I am real, Marshall. Hang on." That night, I made the decision to hold on to God no matter what.

I can't tell you what a powerful difference that decision made in my life. My bitterness was gone, and a peace seemed to wash over me. The change wasn't instantaneous, and I still had rough days just like everyone else, but over time I gained more self-assurance, stopped drinking, cussing, and running after the world's delights. Jesus Christ undoubtedly changed my life. I still have tough days today, but God's Holy Spirit is always with me to help out in my times of need.

Ways To Use Your Testimony

With my experiences, I can talk about the city, public transportation challenges, or rush hour traffic, along with ball games and free public venues for family time. I can talk about rural America and buying my own farm. I can talk about my years in the military, as well as working at a manufacturing plant and the challenges that arise in that environment. I can talk about living in a used, 14 x 70 Windsor (yes, really) mobile home, and initially having a single mattress on the floor for my bed. I can talk about living from meal to meal or times of prosperity. All of these areas merely help me find a possible door of opportunity to share about how God changed my life for the better and helped me in the different seasons of my life. Then I can ask something like this: "Would you like for God to change your life like that?" or "Have you ever thought about a relationship with God like that?"

A downfall of many—including me at times—is failing to ask the question whether someone would like to experience a real relationship with God after we have shared what God has done in our lives. When we do that, it's like holding a rope in your hands as you pull someone to safety, but right when they get to the top you let go! In reality, you would never do this on purpose. However, when we fail to ask folks about where they are with God or whether they have thought about trying to let God help them in their situation, we are failing them. I am not encouraging anyone to manipulate or pressure people—I hate this as much as the next person, but I do think if we care enough about those people whom we have probably built relationships with, then we should at least share something as wonderful as a changed life with them. Sometimes when I'm around a tougher group of folks, I may jokingly question them and say they need to be in church in a non-offensive way to just plant the seed.

With some people you just have to be blunt, so don't be afraid when the Holy Spirit leads you to be candid. Greg Laurie seems to agree with this mindset when he highlights the importance of asking the question: "How do we make that transition from sharing our testimony and the essential Gospel message to actually leading another person to Christ? It's not as hard as you may think. But you have to ask the question sooner or later of the person you are speaking to: 'Would you like to ask Jesus Christ into your heart right now?'"[132] With most people, if we are not clear about what we are asking them to do, the door is wide open for confusion. So, after sharing your testimony, strive to clearly ask the most important question of all.

What about you? Perhaps you have lived a life of affluence and have never worried about money. But you may have endured shallow people who have tried to use or abuse you. You may have felt the emptiness of all that wealth and no true love, friendships, or purpose for your life; all the toys and no real kindness from the world around you. Or, you may be the exact opposite with a life of abuse, alcohol, drugs, and failed relationships. You may have walked through the darker side of humanity and been fortunate enough to live to tell others about it. You may also have been that person raised

---

132 Greg Laurie, *Tell Someone*, Kindle edition, location 1223.

in church who found Jesus Christ at an early age. No matter what your testimony is, it reveals a loving, caring God who not only can deliver us, but who can keep us, change us, give us true love, and a purpose for our lives. He's an awesome God!

I've got to stop for a moment and share some important news with you. Never be ashamed of your testimony! I have talked to people who feel that they don't have a testimony because they were raised in church—but that's a great testimony! God kept you from so many things and allowed you to be in a position to help others who have grown up in the church, yet don't see their real need for a personal relationship with Christ.

Perhaps you feel that your testimony is so bad that you are ashamed of your past. I can totally relate. I ran from God for twelve years and when we run from God—or have never been exposed to Him—there are things of which we're not too proud. But God can use everything that any of us have ever experienced in our lives, whether past, present, or future. We just need to have that mindset that submits to Christ, follows the leading of the Holy Spirit, and never quits trying to help others see the incredible things that God can do in our lives if we let Him. God truly wants to use you as a lifesaver no matter if you are a person of affluence, poverty, or somewhere in between. Keep looking for opportunities to connect with people in hopes of sharing some good news with them—and never quit.

Now It's Your Turn

This may really be a challenge for some of you, but it will be a great challenge to overcome! In writing your own testimony, you basically are writing about three things: Your life before Christ; the events leading up to your decision to follow Christ; and your life after you accepted Jesus Christ as your lord and savior. Do your best to use language that someone who has never heard of Jesus Christ or been in a church can understand. Religious language can be very offensive so do your best to use common, everyday secular language to share your testimony. Alright, here we go!

First, write at least one paragraph to describe the type of person you were before making a decision to follow Christ. What adjectives would describe you as a person? Write down something about the type of family you grew up in and the home life you experienced. What business were you involved in and what business practices did you use that changed after you met Jesus Christ? What activities would you do to be accepted by others, earn money, or just survive? Perhaps you were on the street or involved in something illegal. Be honest and be humble. People notice authenticity.

Second, write at least one paragraph describing the circumstances surrounding the time when you decided to follow Christ. Was there another person involved? Did you have a personal, divine encounter when you were all alone somewhere? Where were you living at the time? Were other relationships influential in your decision—your children or spouse, if married. What was it that helped you realize this thing called Christianity was real? Were you scared? What fears did you have? Did your experience happen at a special camp? In a special church service? Was there a special speaker who preached? Help your listener feel the same feelings you had when you finally came to that point of decision to abandon your past and reach out to Jesus Christ.

Lastly, write at least one paragraph describing how you felt immediately after your decision to ask Jesus Christ to forgive you of your sins and become the Lord of your life. Did you feel something? Did anything change immediately or were your changes more significant later? What is your life like now? What has God done for you that you could have never gotten for yourself? You can share how you are now a part of a pretty awesome family—God's family. After you wrap up telling how your life has changed, don't forget to ask others: "Would you like to experience that kind of relationship with God?" You could also ask a more subtle question like, "Have you ever experienced anything like that?" It's a very general question but asking a question this way allows the Holy Spirit to work on the person with whom you are talking, and it also gives that person an opportunity to respond.

Now that you have written your testimony down, take some time to prayerfully read through it. Imagine sharing that testimony in one minute, several minutes, or for an hour over a cup of coffee with a friend. Keep working on your testimony to add additional information that might be helpful in different settings. When reading your testimony, it may jog your memory about something you forgot, so don't be afraid to continually tweak your testimony and make it better! This is your testimony, and no one can take it away from you. With that said, don't just read your testimony to someone, you must memorize it and make it your own. It's your story and people will be much more likely to respond positively when they see that your testimony is something that comes from your heart—not just your head.

Never quit exploring

Every Christian needs to realize, a serious decision that will change your life for eternity is not a decision made lightly. So, don't be discouraged and quit if someone doesn't decide to let Jesus Christ have Lordship and leadership of their life every time you try to share your faith. "Discouragement can be painfully sharp sometimes as we share this best of news only to have it received as unimportant or unbelievable. But that's where we must remember that it is our part simply to give out the message; God will bring the increase."[133] Keep praying for opportunities and exploring the places you frequent on a daily or weekly basis.

Sometimes, just doing acts of kindness cause people to take notice and provide opportunities for a kind word or the start of a relationship. I've seen people give up their seats on the metro to older people and everyone within eyesight noticed that simple act of kindness. If you ride public transportation every day, your simple acts of kindness may open the door to faith conversations later on. If you visit a certain coffee shop, grocery store, bank, gas station, business, or restaurant on a frequent basis you will get to know those people who work there and other patrons as well. Conversely, they will get to know you too. And if you are a person full of kindness and concern for them, that attitude may just open the door to faith conversations at some point.

As a matter of fact, the old formula for sharing the Gospel message focused a lot on sin and an eternity of life with Christ or punishment. However, the formula we rehearsed typically left out too much of the Gospel. As Dr. George Hunter shared:

> Yes, the Gospel is about second birth and eternal life, but it is also about the love, grace, righteousness, goodness, peace, and kingdom of God. It is also about the forgiveness of sins and freedom from sin; reconciliation and redemption; and justification, abundant life, sanctification, and more. Furthermore, the Gospel includes Jesus' own message that calls us to a new life, this side of death, in which we live no longer for our own will but his; and his message's wider

---

133 Mark Dever, *The Gospel and Personal Evangelism* (Wheaton: Crossway Books, 2007), 111.

themes proclaim a vision of justice, peace, and a redeemed creation.[134]

The Gospel truly touches every aspect of our lives, so trying to cover every detail of that and convince someone of their need to "get saved" in a five-minute window is unrealistic. It not only leaves out some essential aspects of the Gospel message, but also places an unhealthy expectation on those of us trying to share our faith. We can't quit having faith conversations because it is naïve to think every question a non-believer has can be answered in one conversation.

That's why so many surveys reveal that it takes numerous encounters with the Christian faith before someone actually gets to the place where they can make an informed decision about Christianity. How wonderful when you are the last link in a long chain of Christian exposure, and you have the privilege of praying with someone to receive Christ into their lives. But it sets us all up for failure when we make salvation decisions as our sole measure of success. That's like expecting to cross the finish line immediately after the starting gun sounds at a track meet. We are called to run the Christian race well, so our focus should be to share some Gospel seeds whenever and wherever the Holy Spirit nudges us to do so. Being obedient to God's Great Commission is the real goal we all should embrace—one step at a time.

We must prayerfully ask God to show us new ways of sharing the timeless truths of Scripture. The great preacher, John Wesley, gave us some wonderful encouragement in having faith conversations with others:

Wesley coached his people to visit with people in their homes and other places. Wesley taught that conversation

---

134 George G. Hunter III, *The Apostolic Congregation*, 84.

permits us to discern what Gospel themes people are most open to, and it is the way to 'get within' people and to 'suit all our discourse to their several conditions and tempers.' He concluded that conversation is necessary to reach most people.[135]

In reality, we don't need to become some instantly loud, Bible-thumping, and often off-putting proclaimers of the Gospel. In truth, we need to continue to live our lives as a testament to God's grace and look for opportunities to include Christ in our everyday conversations. This lets our actions speak as a clear testament for Christ as we "go about doing good." In doing so, we model Christ Himself. According to Acts 10:38, "how God anointed Jesus of Nazareth with the Holy Spirit and with power. He went about doing good and healing all who were oppressed by the Devil, for God was with him." So too, let us go and do likewise because God is with us as well.

It is helpful to remember that we must all "earn the right" to speak into someone's life at a spiritual level (which is usually a very guarded place in most people's lives). Sometimes we earn that right when our testimony experience connects with others. At other times, earning that right happens over a long period of time as we develop trusted relationships with people we care about. So, don't get frustrated and quit when faith conversations don't seem fruitful—keep exploring the community around you for new ways and methods to share the wonderful story of Christ. Vince Lombardi once said: "Winners never quit, and quitters never win," but we all know that life doesn't always fall into a simple cliché. Sometimes, quitting is exactly what God wants: quitting drugs, sinful behavior, abuse, or any number of other denigrating behaviors. But when it

---

135 George G. Hunter III, *The Apostolic Congregation*, 87.

comes to the Great Commission's mandate of sharing the hope of Christ to a world that is lost without Him, we can rest assured that God does not want us to quit—ever.

Thankfully, we are all merely links in an often-lengthy chain of people trying to lead others to Christ—no one link is more important than another. We are only responsible for our part. God alone knows the heart, and He alone should get all the credit for any good that happens. Surveys indicate that it may take twelve to fifteen or more spiritual encounters before someone can make an informed decision for Christ. So don't get upset when the person you are sharing with doesn't cross that line of faith—you may only be link number nine! God has commanded us to scatter the Gospel seed—He will do the rest. As the Apostle Paul stated, "*I have planted, Apollos watered; but God gave the increase*" (1 Corinthians 3:6 KJV). So, go scatter some seed today and take heart that you are one awesome link!

WHAT'S NEXT?

If you have had the privilege of praying with someone to place their faith in the Lord Jesus Christ, try to give them a Bible or New Testament and encourage them to begin reading it! Many believe that the book of Mark or John may be the best starting point but starting is the key. Also, encourage them to attend a good church. As I mentioned before, try to get a name and contact information so that you can follow up with them or share the information with your church leadership. This way, your church leaders can send relevant follow up resources to them.

Additionally, you need to share the great things that God is doing in your life as you step out in faith. Sharing the little victories that you experience in talking to other people about what God has done in your life will encourage others. Being honest about fears or insecurities that God has helped you overcome will only bless others who are trying to follow Christ's commands.

Most importantly, you and your friends need to thank the One who allowed you to have divine encounters—God Himself. God alone deserves all the glory for any good that comes out of our evangelism efforts—and yes, I know I keep saying that, but it is important! After all, He is the One who sent His Son, Jesus Christ, to take our place on the cross at Calvary. He alone changes hearts. Perhaps today—He has changed yours a little bit too.

THE BATTLE HYMN OF THE REPUBLIC

The following verses of this wonderful hymn, written by Julia Ward Howe in November 1861, were published in the February 1862 edition of *The Atlantic Monthly*. The chorus was added at a later date and apparently uses the music from the song, *John Brown's Body*. These verses remind us that a day of judgment is coming, for which we must prepare, as well as the tremendous cost paid by Christ to set every captive free. May we never forget the price that was paid for each one of us. You are indeed a very special person in God's eyes.

Mine eyes have seen the glory of the coming of the Lord;
He is trampling out the vintage where the grapes of wrath are stored;
He hath loosed the fateful lightning of His terrible swift sword;
His truth is marching on.

I have seen Him in the watch-fires of a hundred circling camps,
They have builded Him an altar in the evening dews and damps;
I can read His righteous sentence by the dim and flaring lamps:
His day is marching on.

I have read a fiery Gospel writ in burnished rows of steel:
"As ye deal with my contemners, so with you my grace shall deal;
Let the Hero, born of woman, crush the serpent with his heel,"
Since God is marching on.

He has sounded forth the trumpet that shall never call retreat;
He is sifting out the hearts of men before His judgment-seat:
Oh, be swift, my soul, to answer Him! be jubilant, my feet!
Our God is marching on.

In the beauty of the lilies Christ was born across the sea,
With a glory in His bosom that transfigures you and me;
As He died to make men holy, let us die to make men free;
While God is marching on.

Chorus
Glory! Glory! Hallelujah!
Glory! Glory! Hallelujah!
Glory! Glory! Hallelujah!
His truth is marching on.

YOUR ASSIGNMENT:
Reflection, Sharing, Application

1. Write your testimony. Remember to write down at least one paragraph: for your life before you made a decision for Christ, when you made a decision for Christ, and your life after you asked Jesus Christ to be the Lord of your life. Remember to use common, secular language.

2. After you have written your testimony, pray through it and memorize it. Add to it as necessary until you feel that it truly reflects the truth. Sometimes, we all have a tendency to forget some things that might be embarrassing or hurtful. We need to be honest and humble.

3. Share your testimony with a friend and get some feedback on how they felt you delivered your story. It's always easier to share back and forth with a friend and hopefully, they can give you some constructive criticism in love that will help you if needed.

CHAPTER 11

NEVER QUIT...WORKING ON YOURSELF

Sharing the Gospel can be a very draining experience for certain people and energizing for others. Some people find it very difficult to start a conversation or publicly share insights into the privacy of their own faith path. For others, it is as natural as breathing. You may identify with one or the other extreme—or be somewhere in between. Unfortunately, many people see evangelism or outreach as an event to conduct. The reality is that we should live a lifestyle of evangelism. Jarram Barrs aptly states: "But what does the Lord want me to do about evangelism in addition to trusting Him for all that I cannot accomplish? He desires that I live in a way that will make the Gospel attractive to all around me."[136] And the key to making the Gospel attractive lies in keeping our hearts in alignment with God.

God has called every follower of Jesus Christ to be a witness, ambassador, or disciple if you will, with all its rights, privileges, and authority. In order to be the kind of true disciple that Christ requires, we must understand the cost and ensure that our own heart is right with God. As has been previously mentioned, this is a

---

136 Jerram Barrs, *The Heart of Evangelism* (Wheaton: Crossway Books, 2001), 55.

daily battle! Jesus helps us see this cost of following Him in a rather shocking response to crowds who were with Him in Luke chapter 14:25-27:

> *Now great crowds accompanied him, and he turned and said to them,* [26] *"If anyone comes to me and does not hate his own father and mother and wife and children and brothers and sisters, yes, and even his own life, he cannot be my disciple.* [27] *Whoever does not bear his own cross and come after me cannot be my disciple.*

I think we would all agree that the position of our heart matters to God, but Jesus' statements are honestly, troubling. We're told in these verses of Scripture that large crowds were traveling with Jesus. Then, Jesus tells the crowd—and us—to hate the people we would normally love the most—even ourselves! Can you imagine Jesus saying to you and your friends, "If anyone comes to me and does not hate father and mother, wife and children, brothers and sisters, yes even their own lives, such a person cannot be my disciple." Boy, that's a difficult Scripture to accept.

So, let's take a closer look at this passage. Jesus says that I have to hate my wife? And my kids? That totally conflicts with other places in Scripture where Jesus has instructed us to honor our parents and love each other—to the point of laying down our lives (John 15:13). These verses don't make sense! It is noteworthy, for us to see that the Greek word used here for hate is *miseō*, pronounced "ma-say-o," and it sounds like something for which I should see a doctor or take medicine. But it literally means to hate, to abhor, or to detest. Frankly, the Scripture uses this word in several places. God even said in Malachi 1:3, "And I hated Esau and laid his mountains and his heritage waste for the dragons of the wilderness." It's a strong word!

But, let's take a walk down memory lane. Remember the story about Rebekah, along with her sons, Jacob and Esau? Esau was born first, Jacob was born second. Yet, God said the first would serve the latter. And don't you think that even before Jacob and Esau were born, God knew what was going to happen. Don't we believe that God has sovereignty, and divine knowledge, so that He knows all things? Sure we do—He's God! As a matter of fact, if we would go to Romans 9:10, Paul is telling the Romans about this story and says that not only does God know, but that Rebekah's children were conceived at the same time by her father Isaac. Yet before the twins were born or had done anything good or bad, in order that God's purpose and "election might stand," not by works, but by him who calls, she was told the older will serve the younger. Verse twelve states: "Just as it is written, Jacob I loved, but Esau I hated."

Wow! I don't know about you, but that's a little hard for me to stomach. That started me digging deeper to resolve a seemingly difficult conflict within the Scriptures. Thankfully, Scripture will bear witness to itself and bring clarity if we'll look hard enough and really want to know the truth. Sometimes when we have a difficulty with a text, we can go to other Scriptures for clarification. This is exactly why we need to look at Matthew 10:37. It's somewhat of a parallel Scripture to our original text in Luke.

You have to understand that in the book of Matthew, the author, and the audience to whom he's writing, are Hebrews. Matthew seems to be a little more educated and articulate in his speech, whereas Luke, who is a physician, is talking to the Greek-speaking world. In Jesus' day, anyone who was not a Hebrew was considered a barbarian. So, Doctor Luke, who is obviously a pretty smart person himself, is trying to write in such a way as to help these folks understand. Matthew, conversely, writes the words of Jesus in this parallel passage with a slightly different wording than our original text. Matthew states: "Anyone who loves their father or mother more than me is not worthy of me. Anyone who loves their son or daughter more than me is not worthy of me. Whoever does not take up their cross and follow me is not worthy of me. Whoever finds their life will lose it, and whoever loses their life for my sake will find it."

Oftentimes in Scripture, the context is crucial. If my daughter, Hannah, and I were driving down the road and I said, "Hey Hannah look at the deer." Unless you are with me you do not know whether I mean one deer or a herd of sixty. You cannot know that unless you are there with Hannah and me. Context is hugely important in ancient documents, and because the Scriptures are so old, one word could oftentimes have numerous meanings depending on the context. So, as we study this, we must understand that this "hate" does not represent all the negative connotations that one could normally associate with the word hate.

How do I know that? Well, for one thing, when we start talking about hate there are a lot of pictures that come to mind. When I hate, that means that I'm usually getting mad or frustrated. This can happen to me while I'm driving, like when people pull out right in front of me! I used to really get livid when that would happen. I wanted to stop them and ask if they even went to driver's education classes! But that is not the case here in Luke's Gospel. Literally, in the original language of the text, Luke is really insinuating that you need to "love less." So, God isn't a hater. He is not contradicting Himself and calling us to hate our families and hate our children, etc. He is calling you and I to love them less than him. Luke is trying to get the Greeks attention—and ours—by using some shocking language.

Another interesting fact is that all the crowds were following Jesus—it seemed as though everyone wanted to touch Jesus! He's a popular guy and healing everybody. Even today, most people would love to brag and include Jesus in their A-list of friends, "Yeah, I was with Jesus again today—we've been friends forever!" And honestly, I'm sure there were lots of people with the same agenda—even in Jesus' day. People were everywhere in the holy city of Jerusalem and wanted to see what He might do next. Then Jesus says, "Look! You want to be my disciple? You want to follow me? Then you have got to love everything else less than me." And in order for the listeners to comprehend the importance of what Jesus is saying, Luke's Gospel account shares slightly different verbiage: "You've got to hate your family. You've got to hate your wife. You've got to hate your children." But literally what he is saying is that you must love them less. It almost ranks right up there with "I hate squash." I'm not mad about it and I don't really hate it—I just don't like it. I used the word hate to convey how strongly I dislike it.

Loving ourselves less than God isn't easy. Neither is loving our parents less than God. You know what else we should love less than God? How about our attitude, our money, our accomplishments, our skills, our position, and even our good looks just to name a few areas. Granted, some folks like me don't have to worry about the good looks issue. But it is so easy for these things to grab hold of us and make themselves a priority. Then, when God comes along and asks us to let it go, we say, "What?!" And we find ourselves holding on a little bit tighter to those things that have distracted us.

We say to ourselves: "That can't be God." But, then when that "sweet, sweet, Spirit" of God, which Doris Akers wrote about years ago, begins to whisper and blow the winds of change in your heart, you're like, "Okay God, it really is you." This song says:

There's a sweet, sweet Spirit in this place
And I know that it's the Spirit of the Lord

When we let that sweet Spirit come into our lives, things change…lives change…hearts change—especially ours. Until we give the Holy Spirit opportunity to come in and change our hearts, we have this potential of getting stuck in a spiritual rut. We start following something or someone we shouldn't. We've said it's o.k. and we've convinced ourselves that it's alright to live on our knees in worship to something besides God. That's not the relational position God intended for you and me to enjoy as disciples, but it's what happens when our hearts are out of position with God. That's why we must never quit working on our relationship with Him.

As a matter of fact, if you lift people or things up above Jesus Christ, that's called idolatry. You're serving something, or someone, else besides God. There are some Christians—for whatever reason—who get distracted. In all honesty, sometimes we all get distracted and take detours. It's a difficult confession, but the enemy of our souls—Satan—is pretty good at what he does. And it's usually not until we're in the presence of God's sweet holy Spirit, that we realize we're not on the path that God wanted us to follow. It's in His presence when God often gives us a glimpse of where we really are in our walk with Him.

You see, God always has a better plan for you and your life than you have. God longs for you and me to love Him more, and it's really His love that prompts us to share our faith with those people who don't know Him. Any "reflection on the love that Paul, Moses, and, above all, Jesus had for people reminds us that the primary motivation for outreach is love."[137] As we strive to love and pursue God more, we'll experience not only His unwavering love for us, but for all of His creation. Honestly, if God is just a means to an end for us and we are just using God to get our blessing, to be on His right side—then we don't really know God. God is not a God to be used and manipulated. He's not some coat that you put on when you want to look good and then take off when you are through with Him. No. God wants to put you on. That's right, God wants to wrap you around Himself and all his goodness in His plan for you. I can almost hear the angels rejoicing when someone gets that

---

137 Barrs, *The Heart of Evangelism*, 27.

relationship with God back in the right position: "Oh my goodness, the family just got bigger!"

God wants us. He wants all of us! That's the only way we can be great ambassadors for Christ. When we have those selfish desires and seek those selfish things to fulfill the desires of our flesh, we seem somehow to always end up disappointed. Or, at least the satisfaction seems to quickly fade and leaves us longing for something else. That's why we must be people of prayer and never quit working on our relationship with God. Then, when the Holy Spirit begins to show us our emptiness without Christ, we'll realize His great gift to us. Oswald Chambers aptly stated, "The only conscious experience those who are baptized in the Holy Ghost will ever have is a sense of absolute unworthiness."[138] Listen to that again: "A sense of absolute unworthiness."

Now, I'm not here to say that we need to beat ourselves down to a point of depression and say: "Well, I'm nobody." Honestly, if we're not careful, we can be prideful in proclaiming our unworthiness. We can pridefully declare how humble we are to all those who will listen! But, that's not God. However, when the "sweet, sweet Spirit" begins to move in our hearts we will all realize that we are not worthy. It's only because of God's grace and mercy, as well as His love that envelopes you and claims you for His own, that He has called us into His family.

I love what theologian, Craig Blomberg, said. He shared: "The foundational motivation for obeying Jesus thus becomes one of profound gratitude for what he has done for us that we could never have performed or deserved on our own. This leads to a radical commitment, a renunciation of our own rights…." And listen to this. "…where the only rewards that are given are to those who are

---

138 Oswald Chambers, *My Utmost For His Highest*, "August 22" (Grand Rapids, MI: Discovery, 1963), 235.

not looking for them."[139] Wow! Let me repeat that last sentence. "The only rewards that are given are to those who are not looking for them."

Are you consumed with being recognized and pursing promotions no matter what the cost? Do you secretly crave acceptance for your achievements from everyone around you? Do you fight for every possible accolade available from others? Well, when you get them, don't expect something else when you get to heaven! Unfortunately, even with all the worldly recognition, you will still be hungry for something else. Because it isn't until we meet Jesus and give one hundred percent of our lives to Him, that He gives us that satisfaction and wholeness. That's why we need a "never quit" attitude that keeps pursuing God and fights to maintain the right spiritual position in spite of all the worldly attractions that come our way.

In running from God for fifteen years, I know all about trying to find satisfaction in popularity, and accolades, and rewards. I could brag about all the accomplishments in my life. I can't really say that I was sent to a military high school because I was such an excellent student! But the reality was that I needed more structure in my life. I went to a great university where I was chosen by my peers to march on the front bugle rank of our band my senior year. That was an incredible privilege. I could just highlight all the great things I did. I could talk about my military experiences. Truly, all of these experiences meant a lot to me personally.

But, guess what? All those things we gain in the world seem to come with a little extra baggage. It all comes with this baggage that isn't very wonderful. There were many things I did not do right when I was estranged from God. There were a lot of mistakes and bad decisions I made when I was running hard in the wrong

---

139 Craig Blomberg, *Jesus and the Gospels: An Introduction and Survey* (Nashville, TN: Broadman & Holman, 1997), 389.

direction. People don't like to brag about their mistakes and bad decisions, do they? I know I don't.

But even when I finally made the decision to pursue Christ, and I gave my life back to the Lord, He shocked me with his goodness. He has taken me more places and allowed me to do more things than I could have ever dreamed, because He had a better plan for my life. God's got a better plan for your life if you'll let Him lead it. Don't think that God's going to take all of the good stuff away. He has something better for you, but you must let God have His way in your life. That's why you can't quit working on "you," and the relationship you have with God.

Even in spite of all the wonderful things that God has done in my life, I realize that I don't deserve it. An incredible price was paid for the spiritual freedoms we all enjoy. And when I think about the price that so many in our country have given for our freedoms; the price they paid—laying down their lives—I'm humbled. Most of us who have been in the military know, the real heroes never came home. Truly, no matter what country you live in, those are the real heroes. Reflecting on them and the sacrifices they made humbles me. Those we see who have limbs missing, are a stark visual reminder that freedom is never free.

My wife, Nancy, bought me a Kirk Cameron movie called *Monumental.* It was about the Puritans who came over to America back in the 1600s. The movie detailed the persecution that they had, how so many of them died or were thrown into prison. Every time they met an obstacle it was just an opportunity to them! They would be excited that God must have something better down the road for them because of all this persecution. For me, the first time I have some kind of hiccup it seems like I'm all down and discouraged about everything and ready to quit. Things are not working the way I think they should. But the Puritans were just the opposite. They were like: "Yeah! We're on the right track! We're all being persecuted!" I don't know about you, but I need that kind of positive attitude more often than not.

Spiritually speaking, God had a plan for the Puritans, and he brought them to America. I think about all the Godly men and women who have gone before us so that we can sit here today and worship God freely in our churches. I'm humbled; and my commitment to preserve freedom grows even more. But when Christ reminds me of the price that He paid, all of my life's achievements—good, bad, or indifferent—all seem to fade. Because I know that I don't deserve His free gift that was so costly to Him. All that Christ has done…harpoons my trophy balloons.

The Lord reminds me often that we're one big family, and I've noticed large families have a tendency to help keep you humble—even in our church families. If you get too full of yourself (or prideful), someone will be more than happy to help bring your attitude back down to earth. When I was growing up, there were four boys and four girls in the Windsor household. Even if you never had siblings, I'm sure you can imagine that we did not have a problem with anyone thinking they were extra special. I had older brothers who would help check your attitude pretty fast. And if they didn't do it my older sisters would step up and help out. And since I was number five of eight children, I also had my younger siblings to help keep me humble.

We all need to remember our humble beginnings without Christ, because this will help us realize how much God loves us. Paul even told the Romans in chapter five verse eight: "But God demonstrates his own love for us in this, while we were still sinners, Christ died for us." And can I tell you, when you begin to realize the sacrifice that God gave for you and me to have that connection with Him, you'll see the unworthiness that Blomberg talked about. Praise God, the veil was torn at the temple. That means I don't need somebody else parleying to Christ for me. I can go to the throne of grace and talk with my savior, Jesus Christ alone. I don't have to pay for access. The cost of admission has already been paid in full.

And because of the love that God has for each of us, He desires to help us. The Psalmist said in Psalm 84:11, "For the Lord is a sun and shield; the Lord bestows favor and honor. No good thing does he withhold from those who walk uprightly." When our heart is in the right position, we'll walk uprightly as God intended—even when sacrifice is involved. That's why it is so important to know the position of your heart, because when sacrifice is involved, it is from the heart, not just your head or your mind.

For example, when you're in the heat of battle, you don't stand around and say: "Well, let's think about this thing and rationalize what we need to do." No, it's what's in your heart that determines your actions. Your instincts take over. Unfortunately, you can't really change your heart. You can work at it, but you can't really change those things in your heart.

Let me give you an example. I could turn to my wife, Nancy, and tell her: "Honey, I don't love you anymore. I'm done. I decided this very moment that I don't love you anymore." I could go through the actions and I could make the decision that I'm going to act as though I don't love her at all anymore. And she would just smile because she knows that is a bunch of silliness. I love my wife! I can't just turn that off—are you kidding me?

I mean we have our tough days, we have arguments. But we also make up! I like making up! Our children don't like it that much, but I like making up. You know I'd much rather there be peace in our home and tranquility in my relationships, but you know what? It's through the struggles of life when the roots grow down deep, and you learn how to hold on through the storm. Some things are worth fighting for, and my marriage is one of them.

Likewise, our relationship with Christ is one of those things worth fighting for. But when you're in the heat of a battle you are driven by the position of your heart—the heart you can't really change. That is why it is so critical for us to know another very important position. That's the position of our head—of our mind—of our thoughts.

When I was a young boy, my mom took me to an agricultural hardware store in our town. It was one of those places that has everything from bird seed to barbed wire—I loved that store! While we were there, I noticed a red, electric car, that was popular and had just come out in the stores. I told my mom that I needed it! This car wasn't as cool as the ones today—it wasn't really remote—it had the wire attached to the car. Nonetheless, it was pretty cutting-edge technology back then. So, when I told my mom I needed that, she said, "Marshall, you need that like you need a hole in your head." I just looked at her and thought, "Really? Is that going to help me?" Because I want that car! If I need a hole, let's get it!

I know some of you are just shaking your heads at me, but some of us need to honestly get our head on straight. You know, we can do something about how we think. What we've let in our minds. As a matter of fact, there was an anonymous writer who said: "Let the mind of the master be the master of your mind." I thought that was pretty wise. We could all benefit by taking that to heart. You see, not every path leads to progress. Even when we're walking hand-in-hand with Jesus, and we're walking down the right path, not all those paths are easy. Some of those paths are hard, and there are times when I let God know I didn't think I was ready for that experience! But God encourages us with His Word, and he also encourages us by so many who have gone before us. That's why we need the saints—the older saints in the body of Christ who can encourage us along this walk called life.

We will all go through a measure of hardship and disappointment, but that doesn't mean we quit. Paul even told that young disciple, Timothy, in 2 Timothy 2:3, "Share in suffering as a good soldier of Christ Jesus." I assure you, Paul did not tell Timothy to endure hardship just because it was the right thing to say. He said it because he knew they were going to endure some difficult times, and the Scriptures bear witness to the hardships and persecution they endured. Philip Yancey shared a powerful truth: "When we stubbornly cling to God in a time of hardship, or when we simply pray, more—much more—may be involved than we ever dream. It requires faith to believe that, and faith to trust that we are never abandoned, no matter how distant God seems."[140] Even in hardship and disappointment, God is still faithful—as He has always been.

John Foxe's book, *Fox's Book of Martyrs,* details some of the heinous things that were suffered by God's chosen ones. For instance, Nero would impale Christians on large spears and set them on fire to light the walkways at his residence. Historical records reveal that there was indeed persecution and hardship. But the Apostle Paul, just like the saints around us today who have gone before us, know that there is a reward when we put all of our faith and trust in the King of glory. He will see us through! Perhaps it is our time to cross over from this life to the next. Perhaps your work here on earth is done. That's okay. Let's run the race that God has set before us! Let's run it with all that is within us and never quit praying for opportunities to share the hope that God has given each of us, because eternity lies in the balance.

Now, how many of you know that the Devil is a liar? If we really believe that he is a liar and the father of it (John 8:44), then why is it that we often listen to him when he whispers sweet enticements in our ears? He will always lead us down a path that feels so right but ends so wrong. When we disengage our minds and let our feelings lead us, we will often be disappointed. It reminds me of a situation that happened between Nancy and me.

---

140 Philip Yancey, *Disappointment With God* (Grand Rapids, MI: Zondervan, 1988), 237.

We have this love-hate relationship. Sometimes I say something to her about social media and the time she spends on it. Then she turns and responds to me saying, "Well, you're on the computer too much." Which I am guilty of doing. I admit it. I am a recovering workaholic. I used to do computer support, so working on a computer is my default work tool. The truth is that we're probably both guilty at times of spending too much time on social media and computers.

But this one night I was really upset for some reason. I was mad but did not say anything. I was working on a sermon, and so you know who was trying to work on me! So, I go to bed early and I'm mad. I'm trying to sleep and mad as a wet hen (an old farmer's expression that means—yep—I was mad). As a matter of fact, I remember that I was sweating I was so mad!

I was laying there in bed sweating and praying. You can take my word for it that my prayers were not very spiritual at that moment. But honestly, I was trying to seek God and find some peace and help with all the other things that were going on at the time. It seemed like my plate was overflowing and I just needed God to help me in my time of weakness and anger.

> "…your decisions will inevitably determine your direction. The position of your mind is one thing you can change."

Then, it was like the Holy Spirit just reached down and spoke to me. We had a dialog like I've never had before. He said,

"You know what Marshall…you're a man of prayer. You honestly pray, don't you?"

"Yes sir," I responded. (You always know that God is setting you up for something when He starts asking you questions to which He already knows the answers!)

The Holy Spirit continued, "Nancy's a woman of prayer. She prays, doesn't she?"

"Yes sir," I responded again.

He said, "Don't you think that you both would hear me if I spoke?"

"Yeah…I guess that's right." I responded sheepishly…knowing that God was right.

And as soon as the Holy Spirit said that to me, because I wanted my heart to be right and I wanted to hear from Him, the fire of my anger was gone. The spiritual smoke from the fire—even the smell of smoke was gone. I mean all the anger I had just been dealing with was instantly gone, and the Lord helped me to think in my mind rightly. Oftentimes we let the enemy stir us up, and when we start getting hurt, we start going down that trail of wanting things our own way. We become determined that our way is the best way, and no one is going to deter us from having it our way.

Sadly, the truth is that we should have gotten down on our knees in our prayer closet and begin to bombard heaven, letting God speak to everyone involved. That night, God graciously spoke to me and I know he will speak to you if you really want to hear Him. It was such a powerful experience for me that I had to get back out of bed and finish my message. That's how awesome God is—He cares enough about me, and you, to reach down and speak to everyone.

Can I tell you something? Decision determines direction. Our decisions will determine our direction in life, but that's not always easy because our feelings get involved! They become huge hurdles. When we get hurt and wounded emotionally, the last thing we feel like doing is sitting down over a cup of coffee or something and saying, "Hey, let's just talk about this." Or pretend that everything is just great, and we're not hurt at all. Like when we come to church, and someone asks us, "How are you doing?" And we respond: "Great!"

Hurt feelings are really difficult to overcome, but can I share a truth with you? Going faster in the wrong direction is not going to get you where you need to go. You and I must make that mental decision to go in the right direction, because decisions will determine direction. It's difficult to reflect the love and attitude of Christ when we are out of sorts with others. I even have relationships that still have not worked out no matter how hard I try, but I just have to leave those in God's hands. The important thing is to make sure the position of my mind and heart are aligned with God. It's okay for the people around you to know that Christians don't have all the answers and we're not perfect. We face hard things in life too, but we've decided to follow Christ—our advocate who intercedes for us. Rest assured, deciding to go in the right direction is the first step to arriving at your destination.

When I was in the military, I used to lead a lot of convoys. Today, you may see convoys on the highways when you are out driving. Seeing them normally leads to a wonderful discussion about how wonderful our military is and how cool it is to see them traveling on the highways. But the truth is that convoys for military maneuvers almost never happen in the daytime. They happen at night. As a matter of fact, you don't even get to turn your regular lights on. The military has something called black-out drive—which really means you should not be driving!

But seriously, the only lights you can use are like penlights. You have some in the front and some red ones in the back. You can imagine how difficult it might be trying to drive under those conditions. As a matter of fact, living in East Texas with all of our pine trees reminds me of my time in Germany. They have pine trees that grow so tall and thick together that you cannot even see the sky at night. No moon. No stars. Nothing.

Additionally, when a military convoy is cruising at night, we hardly ever went anywhere on a main, paved road. If we did it was only until we could get to the next gravel or dirt road. You are out in the middle of nowhere! Ironically, military maps seem to have roads that no one else has. Sometimes, you are so frustrated that you are wondering who drew that "stupid" map, because you could swear that there is no road where that map says there should be one.

One night I was leading a convoy across some difficult terrain and we arrived at a T-Intersection on a gravel road. I couldn't see the hand in front of my face, and I am supposed to figure out where we need to go in order to rendezvous with the other vehicles in our unit. Now, the last thing you want to do is to get lost. Incidentally, people who lead convoys would never confess to being lost either— they would just say they were "temporarily misoriented." I admit, I did not want to join the ranks of those who had gotten temporarily misoriented, so I grabbed my flashlight and got out of my jeep to make a closer inspection of the T-Intersection. I am down on my knees looking for tire tracks, because I did not want to get lost!

In all honesty, no one likes to get lost or temporarily misoriented. But the truth remains, for us to know where we're going, we often need a little illumination—no matter if you are in the secular or spiritual arena. As a Christian, that also means our illumination is not always just light, because we often need some spiritual illumination. The Psalmist tells us in Psalm 119:105, "Thy word is a lamp unto my feet and a light unto my path." The Word of God will illuminate the answer when we face difficulties—the dark places in our lives. It will help us get to the other side. That is why we need to read and study the word of God for ourselves. It will also help provide divine direction and dialog in the midst of faith conversations. Knowing the Scripture can actually help us in our outreach efforts by encouraging us personally and equipping us with relevant Scriptures to share.

In the military, or even at home, if you have all the weapons or resources in the world but don't know how to use them, how are they going to help you? I read a quote in the Infantry Journal once that said: "When you pull the pin, Mr. Grenade is no longer your friend." They are telling you in a somewhat humorous way that you need to get rid of that grenade! There is only so much time after you release the lever until the grenade explodes. When you pull the pin and release the lever is not the time to ask, "How much time do I have?" And if you turn around to ask your friends, you will find yourself a very lonely person. If those friends are smart, they are gone!

As a Christian, if you do not know the Word of God that's sharper than any two-edged sword (Hebrews 4:12), you cannot use it against the attacks of the enemy of your soul. God has given us His word and He longs for us to study it and know it in our hearts. It's a great gift and stands as the most powerful resource we have in sharing our faith with those around us.

Another great gift is God's Holy Spirit. I love the presence of the Holy Spirit and being led by Him because he helps us act like Christians with unbelievers. Richard Blackaby stated:

> One reason Christians fail to show grace to unbelievers is that we subconsciously believe everyone should share our values. We Christians tend to form our own subculture. We spend most of our time with other Bible believers. We develop a common lingo and lifestyle. When we interact with those who do not accept Christ's teachings or His Lordship, we are flabbergasted. The reality, though, is that unbelieving people can be expected to act only one way—as unbelievers.[141]

The Holy Spirit is the one who gives us grace in dealing with others, corrects our attitudes, and reminds us of Scriptures, articles, or books we have studied or read in years past. It's also the Holy Spirit who gives us those gentle nudges to start conversations or ask divine questions. The Holy Spirit not only helps you in your efforts to reach out, but also strengthens right decisions and a mindset

---

141 Richard Blackaby, *Putting A Face on Grace: Living A Life Worth Passing On* (Sisters, OR: Multnomah, 2006), 125.

of "never quit." He is the one who helps us act in a Christlike manner—even when we face hardships and disappointments that can be crippling.

The Apostle Paul shares in 1 Timothy 6:12, "Fight the good fight of faith. Lay hold on eternal life, whereunto thou art also called and hath professed a good profession before many witnesses." Paul is telling Timothy, "Don't just tell people you are a Christian. Why don't you act like it?" Christ continues to admonish every one of us as well, to quit telling people you are a Christian and start acting like it. People need to see a change in you that causes them to say, "Hey, there's something different about you. What's going on in your life?" Then you can say, "I've just had the most incredible, life-changing event happen to me. I recently made a decision to follow Jesus Christ and He has changed my life." Your actions alone can lead to some really incredible faith conversations.

Your actions will give you away every time, no matter what you tell other people. We don't need to fake it until we make it. We need to give our whole heart and life to Jesus Christ. As I shared earlier, our decision doesn't mean that we hate or discard our family responsibilities. It means that we do not put anything above God. There is no way you can put other things before God and then expect God to change your life like He desires. God said that if you put other things above Him then you cannot be His disciple. The Gospel of Matthew tells us that we are not worthy of being His disciple when we put other things above God: Our family, our job, our position, our money, our status, our talents, or any other thing that can keep us from Jesus Christ. All of these must be nailed to our cross that God has called you and I to pick up and carry daily.

What did Luke 14:27 tell us? "And whoever does not carry their cross and follow me cannot be my disciple." Those things that keep us from Christ are what we have to nail to the cross every day. Jesus nailed every sin known to humankind to the cross that He bore, and we've got to nail everything that would interrupt and hinder our relationship with Jesus Christ to the cross that we willingly bear for Him.

God created you to have an awesome life full of joy and purpose, which includes telling other people about Him. Jesus said in John 15:11, "These things have I spoken unto you that my joy might remain in you and that your joy might be full." God's hope, joy, peace, provision, deliverance, protection, and all the other attributes of God are available to every follower of Christ. He is just waiting for us to finally lay down our agendas and our plans, and everything else we have mapped out, and say, "Okay God, I'm ready for your plan. I'm available."

You see, we each have to get our head in the right position by making a decision to let Christ have everything in our lives. Every. Single. Thing. That decision determines our direction and gives God the opportunity to change the position of our hearts. Honestly, position really does matter to God. It's what allows you and I the freedom to stand up and follow Christ—becoming the ambassador He so desires. When we allow Jesus Christ the opportunity to truly change our lives, we'll begin to realize the hope that is now within us—and that's a hope worth sharing.

BLESSED ASSURANCE[142]

Blessed assurance, Jesus is mine!
Oh, what a foretaste of glory divine!
Heir of salvation, purchase of God,
Born of His Spirit, washed in His blood.

Refrain:
This is my story, this is my song,
Praising my Savior all the day long;
This is my story, this is my song,
Praising my Savior all the day long.

Perfect submission, perfect delight,
Visions of rapture now burst on my sight;
Angels, descending, bring from above
Echoes of mercy, whispers of love.

Perfect submission, all is at rest,
I in my Savior am happy and blest,
Watching and waiting, looking above,
Filled with His goodness, lost in His love.

---

142 The lyrics of this wonderful hymn of the church, *Blessed Assurance*, were written by
    Frances (Fanny) J. Crosby, who was blind, in 1873. Her friend Phoebe Knapp wrote
    the music.

SUMMARY

Well now you know about L.E.A.R.N. Evangelism! Listen to the leading of the Holy Spirit. Engage others in conversations. Ask questions that might lead to faith conversations. Relay the message of Jesus Christ and what he's done in your life. And most importantly, never quit working on yourself and praying for opportunities to have divine appointments that lead to even more faith conversations. Remember all the positive nicknames you may be remembered for: hero, lifesaver, compassionate, loving, friend, and a host of other adjectives that are merely a reflection of the wonderful Holy Spirit of Almighty God that resides in you! I am so excited for the spiritual conversations that await you and which are so desperately needed. Here's why.

I recently had a terrible dream that truly disturbed me. I was at a party of sorts with some friends (I thought). The festivities were catered by another company and we were all sitting around laughing and having a good time. When the catering people showed up, we discussed what was expected and where they should set up. The atmosphere was jovial with some people drinking and some not. All through the dream I seemed to be separated, yet a part of the crowd—an observer if you will.

When the catering folks went inside their container-type building to start getting ingredients, food, and drinks together, a terrible thing happened. One of my supposed friends went down and put a lock on the building. They proceeded to laugh about it and one friend asked another if he had a match. In horror, I watched as they proceeded to set the container building on fire! The catering folks were pounding on the door and the folks I knew were just laughing about what they had done. No one tried calling for help.

The festivities were located in the country and help was far away. When I asked my friends if they weren't going to call for help, they told me that I could call someone if I wanted. I ran over to the wall, where a phone was hanging and asked if anyone knew who to call for help. No 911 emergency service number existed where we were, but someone said that there was an ambulance service not too far away. When I tried calling them, it became apparent that the ambulance crew were on another call and could not come. I was too late! I was totally in shock and dismay at the people who had been in the building, which was now totally engulfed in flames. I knew the possibility of helping any survivors at this point was gone. Suddenly, my alleged friends decided that the fun was over, so they hopped in their vehicles and left.

It was at this point that I woke up feeling so grieved in my spirit and praying at the same time. I began asking the Lord what this meant, and He began to reveal some surprising things. The friends in the dream, were actually Satan and his servants. They were sitting back laughing because they had deceived those honest, hardworking caterers, who were just there because they were doing their job as part of the party. I was so distraught by the sound of laughter from those who pretended to be friends— concerning the death of so many. They were drinking and making fun of the people who were being burned alive. A terrible vision for me personally.

But the Lord began to reveal how we often go through life not thinking about eternity or the friends we have who represent those hard-working caterers. We sit back and let them enter eternity without telling them the importance of making a decision about their faith paths, or the difference that a relationship with Jesus Christ can make. So, we sit back and try so hard to fit in with the world and its standard of acceptance—the supposed friends in my dream. Then, when the fire is burning, and the door is locked, we try to call for help and tell someone.

That is indeed a noble effort, but an effort far too late to help anyone. If someone had just warned the caterers—our neighbors, our real friends, our family, our colleagues, our peers, our classmates, the people we encounter everyday—their fate of being burned alive and being separated from God for eternity might have been averted. If someone would have been obedient to share the joys and hope that Christ gives to every believer, things might have been different. Thankfully, with my obedience and yours, those caterers in our lives can have the chance to make a decision to enjoy eternity in the presence of an amazing God. Our obedience will help them hear about a Divine Creator who loves them so much, that His only Son laid down His life for them. Then they too, can have the ultimate peace with the Giver of all life. God is just waiting to use you and me in the greatest adventure on the planet—the adventure of sharing the hope that is within us. I pray that you will indeed answer His call to do so.

AMAZING GRACE[143]

Amazing grace! How sweet the sound
That saved a wretch like me!
I once was lost, but now am found;
Was blind, but now I see.

'Twas grace that taught my heart to fear,
And grace my fears relieved;
How precious did that grace appear
The hour I first believed.

Through many dangers, toils and snares,
I have already come;
'Tis grace hath brought me safe thus far,
And grace will lead me home.

The Lord has promised good to me,
His Word my hope secures;
He will my Shield and Portion be,
As long as life endures.

Yea, when this flesh and heart shall fail,
And mortal life shall cease,
I shall possess, within the veil,
A life of joy and peace.

The earth shall soon dissolve like snow,
The sun forbear to shine;

---

143 The lyrics to *Amazing Grace* were originally written by John Newton and published
in 1779.

But God, who called me here below,
Will be forever mine.

When we've been there ten thousand years,
Bright shining as the sun,
We've no less days to sing God's praise
Than when we'd first begun.

ACKNOWLEDGEMENTS

This book would not have happened except for the tireless efforts of Dr. Kitty Bickford and her team at Chalfant Eckert Publishing. Many thanks to Jim, mom, and so many others who pitched in to help make this vision a reality.

Thanks too, for all of those who have graciously allowed me to share the hope that I cherish until the day that I actually get to see my Savior face-to-face. So many have gone to heaven before me and I pray that multitudes will follow me should the Lord tarry.

Most importantly, I want to thank my wife, Nancy, and daughter, Hannah, for all of their encouragement and grace during my times of moodiness while trying to meet self-appointed deadlines. My son Joshua's and Nancy's proofreading has saved me much embarrassment, and my readers untold agony. May God's blessings shower down upon my children, as well as my very best friend and prayer partner.

ABOUT THE AUTHOR

Marshall Moore Windsor was born in Dallas, Texas, but spent much of his early years on the family farm in Missouri. A love of the outdoors and no stranger to hard work, Marshall pitched in with his seven siblings to help keep the family farm running. Fishing and frog hunting were some of his favorite pastimes when he wasn't cleaning horse stalls, hauling hay, working cattle, or helping get crops in or out of the fields.

Marshall graduated from Kemper Military School and Texas A&M University with a BS in Mechanized Agriculture prior to entering the United States Army as a Field Artillery officer in 1983. It was during Marshall's time in military service that he rededicated his life to God.

Marshall and Nancy sold their farm in 1999 and moved to Springfield, Missouri to attend the one-year Bible program at Central Bible College and step out into evangelistic ministry. Marshall received both his Master of Divinity degree in the area of biblical languages and his Doctor of Ministry degree in the area of evangelism and discipleship from The Assemblies of God Theological Seminary. Marshall served as an adjunct professor of evangelism from 2007 to 2011 at Central Bible College and currently serves in that role at the Assemblies of God Theological Seminary in Springfield, Missouri, and SUM Bible College and Theological Seminary in El Dorado Hills, California. Marshall and Nancy transitioned to East Texas where they reside with their family and base their ministry today.

In 2005 Marshall was appointed as the National Evangelist Representative for the Assemblies of God fellowship and served as the Evangelist General Presbyter for over thirteen years. Marshall and his family have ministered around the world for over twenty years and continue to partner with churches in their evangelism efforts, as well as teach and train young evangelists, in order to fulfill God's Great Commission.

Resources to help enrich your life and help you in sharing your faith journey with others.

Becoming A Spirit-Empowered Evangelist

Have you ever wrestled with how to become a full-time, vocational evangelist after God calls you to that area of ministry? Or wondered what itinerant ministers endure so that you can pray specifically for them? Follow Dr. Windsor as he shares the truths that he and his family discovered over their many years of ministry. From scheduling and family life to working with missionaries overseas, you'll find nuggets of truth that will help shape your ministry and enrich your life.

*Available in paperback, eBook, and hardbound versions!

L.E.A.R.N. Evangelism: Giving Away the Greatest Gift

Pocket sized booklets are small, 28-page booklets that provide opportunities to carry the L.E.A.R.N. Evangelism sharing tool with you wherever you go.

Also available in eBook format, this booklet lets you read and reread—in about 30 minutes—the tips on sharing the hope that is within you. God longs to bring others into a right relationship with Him, and He may just want to use you to do that! We all have a story about what God has done in our lives, and your story may just be THE story that helps change another person's life for eternity.

**Bulk quantity discounts on paperback versions available for pastors.

Aprenda A Evangelizar is the L.E.A.R.N. Evangelism booklet for all our Spanish readers. *Available in paperback and eBook versions!

**Bulk quantity discounts on paperback versions available for pastors.

**Visit http://www.marshallwindsor.com or http://www.windsmin.org to find out more about these timely resources.

Want to schedule a workshop?
Send us an email at **mail@windsmin.org**

Note from the Publisher

Are you a first time author?

Not sure how to proceed to get your book published?
Want to keep all your rights and all your royalties?
Want it to look as good as a Top 10 publisher?
Need help with editing, layout, cover design?
Want it out there selling in 90 days or less?

Visit our website for some exciting new options!